KN261 RID

D0182977

KEY FACTS

COMPANY
LAW

ANN RIDLEY

UNIVERSITY OF BRISTOL
LIBRARY

3 0 AUG 2012

WITHDRAWN

Hodder & Stoughton

A MEMBER OF THE HODDER HEADLINE GROUP

Orders: please contact Bookpoint Ltd, 130 Milton Park, Abingdon, Oxon OX14 4SB.
Telephone: (44) 01235 827720. Fax: (44) 01235 400454. Lines are open from 9.00–6.00,
Monday to Saturday, with a 24-hour message answering service.
Email address: orders@bookpoint.co.uk

British Library Cataloguing in Publication Data
A catalogue record for this title is available from The British Library.

ISBN 0 340 84586 4

First published 2002
Impression number   10 9 8 7 6 5 4 3 2
Year   2005 2004 2003

Copyright © 2002 Ann Ridley

All rights reserved. No part of this publication may be reproduced or transmitted in any form
or by any means, electronic or mechanical, including photocopy, recording, or any information
storage and retrieval system, without permission in writing from the publisher or under licence
from the Copyright Licensing Agency Limited. Further details of such licences (for
reprographic reproduction) may be obtained from the Copyright Licensing Agency Limited, of
90 Tottenham Court Road, London W1T 4LP.

Cover design by Stewart Larking
Typeset by Transet Limited, Coventry, England.
Printed in Great Britain for Hodder & Stoughton Educational, a division of Hodder Headline
Plc, 338 Euston Road, London NW1 3BH by Cox & Wyman Ltd, Reading, Berks.

CONTENTS

PREFACE

The Key Facts series is a practical and complete revision aid that can be used by students of law courses at all levels from A Level to degree and beyond, and in professional and vocational courses.

The Key Facts series is designed to give a clear view of each subject. This will be useful to students when tackling new topics and is invaluable as a revision aid. Most chapters open with an outline in diagram form of the points covered in that chapter. The points are then developed in a structured list form to make learning easier. Supporting cases are given throughout by name and, for some complex areas, facts are given to reinforce the point being made.

The Key Facts series aims to accommodate the syllabus content of most qualifications in a subject area, using many visual learning aids.

Company law may be a module of both law and business studies degree courses. It is also a vital subject in many professional and vocational courses. The detail and complexities of the subject can make it difficult for the student. This book aims to help students throughout their course.

The law is as I believe it to be on 1st February 2002.

CASES

CHAPTER 1

COMPANY FORMATION

1.1 INCORPORATION

Formalities:
- Business Names
- Memorandum of Association
- Articles of Association
- supporting documents
- prescribed fee

Certificate of Incorporation provides evidence
- that requirements of the Act have been fulfilled
- that the company is a plc (if that is the case)

INCORPORATION

Duties of promoters:
Statute:
- misrepresentation in prospectus
Common law:
- negligence
- deceit
Fiduciary:
- good faith
- fair dealing
- disclosure

Pre-incorporation contracts
- liability of agent who purports to make contract on behalf of company prior to incorporation
  - Art 9 First Company Law Directive
  - s36C CA 1985

1. A company may be created by registration of documents with the Registrar of Companies under the Companies Act 1985, registration with another public official or body (e.g. under the Charities Act 1993), by statute or by Royal Charter. We are concerned only with the first method, that is, with 'registered companies'.

2. The most significant consequence, to a lawyer, of incorporation is that a company is recognised in law as a legal person.

3. The Limited Liability Partnership Act 2000 allows the incorporation by registration of a limited liability partnership for 'carrying on a lawful business with a view to profit'. Note that a company can be registered for non-business purposes.

4. A company may be limited or unlimited: the vast majority are limited, which means that individual shareholders are not directly responsible for the debts of the company.

5. Furthermore, a number of different types of company may be registered, the most important distinction being between public companies and private companies.

Public companies	Private companies
Defined by s1(3) CA 1985	No statutory definition
Limited by shares	May be limited by shares or by guarantee, or unlimited
Must have at least two members	May be formed with only one member
Minimum share capital – s11	No minimum share requirements
Designated by 'plc' or Welsh equivalent	If limited, must include 'Limited' or 'Ltd' after name
Shares may be offered to the public	Shares may not be offered to the public – note consequences of this

1.2 REGISTRATION

1.2.1 Documentation

1. To incorporate a company it is necessary to deliver to the Registrar of Companies for England and Wales or, for a company to be registered in Scotland, the Registrar of Companies for Scotland the Memorandum of Association and Articles of Association (s10 CA 1985).
2. The Memorandum of Association must contain:
   - company name;
   - country of registered office;
   - objects clause;
   - limitation of liability clause;
   - capital clause (the amount of the company's capital and its division into shares of a fixed nominal amount);
   - association clause.
3. Articles of Association (may be in the form of Table A).
4. There must be supporting documents:
   - statement of initial capital;
   - notice of intended situation of registered office;
   - declaration that statutory requirements regarding incorporation have been complied with.
5. Prescribed fee must be paid.

1.2.2 Registrar's role

1. The Registrar then issues a Certificate of Incorporation, which is conclusive evidence
   - that the requirements of the Act in respect of registration and of matters precedent and incidental to it have been complied with, and that the association is a company authorised to be registered, and is duly registered under the Act; and
   - if the certificate contains a statement that the company is a public company, that the company is such a company.

2. The Registrar cannot refuse registration if the objects of the company are lawful, the documents are in order and the name is acceptable according to the Business Names Act 1985 (*R v Registrar of Companies, ex p Bowen* (1914); *R v Registrar of Companies, ex p A.G.* (1980) reported (1991).

3. A refusal by the Registrar to register a company is subject to judicial review.

4. Note also that it is possible to buy a company 'off the shelf'.

1.3 PROPOSALS FOR REFORM

The Company Law Steering group have proposed that :
- the memorandum and articles of association should be replaced by a single constitution;
- one member should be allowed to form any kind of company;
- members of a company would be able to change the constitution by special resolution, but would also be able to 'entrench' certain provisions;
- companies formed under new legislation would have unlimited capacity.

1.4 PROMOTERS

1. The term promoter is one of fact, not of law. A promoter has been defined as: 'One who undertakes to form a company with reference to a given project and to set it going, and who takes the necessary steps to accomplish that purpose.' (Cockburn C.J., *Twycross v Grant* (1877))

2. People who act in a purely administrative capacity (e.g. solicitors/accountants) are *not* promoters.

3. Promoters working together to set up a company are not necessarily partners (*Keith Spicer v Mansell* (1970)).

1.4.1 Duties of a promoter

1. There are no statutory duties on a promoter, except in respect of untrue statements made in a prospectus.

2. In Equity a promoter owes a fiduciary duty to the company when it is incorporated. The essence of this duty is in 'good faith, fair dealing and full disclosure'.

3. Some problems arise as to how and to whom disclosure should be be made.

   a) It was suggested that disclosure must be to an independent board of directors;

   b) but this may not be possible in the case of many private companies, where the promoters may become the directors of the company;

   c) disclosure to the members as a whole has long been recognised as effective (*Erlanger v New Sombrero Phosphate Co* (1878); (*Gluckstein v Barnes* (1900)).

4. At common law the promoter is probably liable in tort for fraud or negligence causing loss to the company.

5. Remedies of the company include:
   - rescission of contract entered into as a result of non-disclosure or misrepresentation;
   - recovery of any secret profit;
   - imposition of constructive trust;
   - damages for breach of fiduciary duty (*Re Leeds & Hanley Theatres* (1902) but the scope of this remedy is somewhat uncertain) and
   - damages for deceit.

6. The law relating to duties of promoters is now of little practical importance as far as public companies are concerned, as a result of legal regulation and the Stock Exchange listing rules. It may still have some relevance to private companies.

1.5 PRE-INCORPORATION CONTRACTS

1. The company, once incorporated, is recognised by the law as a separate legal person. As such it can act only through agents (see Chapter 4). Agency problems arise where a person purports to make a contract for a company *prior* to incorporation.

2. A contract made on behalf of a company before its incorporation does not bind the company, nor can it be enforced or ratified by the company after incorporation. Early cases distinguished between contracts made 'for and on behalf of' the company (*Kelner v Baxter* (1866)), and those where the promoter signed his own name to authenticate the name of the company (*Newborne v Sensolid* (1954)).

3. The fine distinctions suggested by these and other cases made the position at common law quite complex. This has, however, been superseded by statute.

4. The First Company Law Directive art. 9 provides:
   'If, before a company being formed has acquired legal personality, action has been carried out in its name and the company does not assume the obligations arising from such action, the persons who acted shall, without limit, be jointly and severally liable therefore unless otherwise agreed.'

5. This was implemented in section 36C CA 1985 which provides:
   'A contract which purports to be made by or on behalf of a company at a time when the company has not been formed has effect, subject to any agreement to the contrary, as one made with the person purporting to act for the company or as agent for it, and he is personally liable on the contract accordingly.'

6. This section was interpreted in *Phonogram v Lane* (1982) in which it was held:
   - the section applies whenever a contract is made prior to incorporation, and fine distinctions as to whether the agent signs on behalf of, or as the company will not be made;
   - the section applies whether the process of incorporation has been started or not (i.e. it is not necessary for the company to be in the course of being formed);
   - the section applies whether or not the company is eventually incorporated.

7. Two recent first instance decisions have further clarified the law:

   a) In *Hellmuth, Obata & Kassabaum Inc v Geoffrey King* (unreported 2000), it was held that the word 'contract' extends to quasi-contractual obligations as well. This interpretation of s36C is consistent with the wording of the First Company Law Directive.

   b) Until recently it was unclear whether an agent would be able to enforce a contract under s36C. This issue was addressed in *Braymist Ltd v Wise Finance Ltd* (2001) and it was held that where s36C applies, a fully effective contract is deemed to have been concluded between the purported agent and the contracting party, conferring both liability and a right of action on the purported agent. This decision is consistent with the wording of the section and with the principle of mutuality – a person who is liable on a contract should also have a right to enforce it.

8. Although s36C has done much to clarify the law, there is still an important defect in that companies cannot ratify pre-incorporation contracts after incorporation. It has now been established that s36C fails to fully implement the Directive (*Braymist Ltd v Wise Finance Ltd*).

9. The section has limitations:

   a) it will not apply when a company has been bought off the shelf and is in the process of changing its name (*Oshkosh B'Gosh Inc v Dan Marbel Inc Ltd* (1989));

   b) the agent must 'purport' to make the contract on behalf of a company and the section will not apply if the parties are unaware that a company has been dissolved (*Cotronic v Dezonie* (1991)).

CHAPTER 2
CORPORATE PERSONALITY

2.1 INTRODUCTION

1. Issue of the certificate of incorporation is conclusive evidence that all the requirements of the Companies Act 1985 in relation to incorporation have been complied with (s13 CA 1985).
2. By incorporation, the company acquires separate legal personality, that is, the company is recognised as a person separate from its members, a principle established in *Salomon v Salomon & Co Ltd* (1897).
3. A registered company created under foreign law is also recognised as a separate legal person in the UK (*Arab Monetary Fund v Hashim (No 3)* (1991)).

2.2 CONSEQUENCES OF INCORPORATION

1. The company is an association of its members and a person separate from its members.
2. The company can make contracts.
3. The company can sue and be sued.
4. The company can own property.
5. The company continues in existance despite change of membership.
6. The shareholders can delegate management to directors.

2.3 ADVANTAGES AND DISADVANTAGES

1. Not everyone agrees that the concept of separate legal identity of companies is generally beneficial. Professor Kahn-Freund

described the decision in *Salomon v Salomon* as 'calamitous'.

2. It sometimes happens that the rule operates against the interests of members (*Tunstall v Steigmann* (1962); *Macaura v Northern Assurance* (1925)).

3. The corporate form may also, in certain circumstances be used by members to avoid liability.

4. On the other hand the view may be taken that if the formalities set out in the Companies Act are followed and the company's purpose is lawful, once the certificate of incorporation is duly issued, the incorporators are entitled to the benefit of separate personality and the motives which lie behind incorporation are irrelevant. This facilitates risk allocation.

2.4 JUDICIAL AFFIRMATION OF THE CONCEPT OF SEPARATE IDENTITY: SOME EXAMPLES

The principle of separate legal personality has been described by Professor Sealy as 'the cornerstone of company law'. The principle is affirmed in the cases below.

1. *Macaura v Northern Assurance* (1925): shareholder had no insurable interest in property owned by the company. However, in the Canadian case *Constitution Insurance Company of Canada v Kosmopoulos* (1987) the court found for the shareholder on similar facts.

2. *Foss v Harbottle*: a member cannot bring an action to redress a wrong done to the company – note exceptions to the rule and see Chapter 10.

3. *Lee v Lee's Air Farming* (1961): a company can employ one of its members who will have all statutory and other rights against the company.

4. *Secretary of State for Trade and Industry v Bottrill* (1999): a sole shareholder can be employed by the company and will have rights under the Employment Rights Act 1996.

2.5 LIFTING THE VEIL

1. The notion that a company is recognised as a person separate from its members is often described as the 'veil of incorporation'.
2. One of the principles of separate legal personality is that the company itself, rather than its members or directors is liable on its contracts.
3. However, in certain circumstances the veil of incorporation has been lifted both judicially and by statute to reveal the reality of who owns and controls the company.

2.5.1 Judicial approaches

1. The courts have been prepared to lift the veil in certain circumstances, but the approach has not been consistent and there is no clear view as to when the courts will be prepared to lift the veil and when they will decline to do so.

	veil lifted	veil not lifted
Evasion of liability, fraud, 'facade'		
Gilford Motors v Horne	x	
Jones v Lipman	x	
Adams v Cape Industries		x
National security		
Daimler v Continental Tyres	x	
Agency		
FG (Films) Ltd	x	
Firestone Tyre and Rubber Co	x	
Smith Stone & Knight v Birmingham Corp	x (but case much criticised)	
R H Rayner		x
Adams v Cape Industries		x
Single economic unit (groups of companies)		
DHN v Tower Hamlets	x	
The Albazero	x	
Woolfson v Strathclyde		x
Re Southard & Co Ltd		x
Adams v Cape Industries		x
To achieve justice		
Re A company (1985)	x	
Adams v Cape Industries		x

2. The Companies Act itself provides that the veil should be lifted in certain circumstances (see below) and the courts have also interpreted provisions in other statutes so as to require that the veil should be lifted.

3. However, in *Dimbleby & Sons Ltd v National Union of Journalists* (1984) it was held that Parliamentary intention that the veil should be lifted must be expressed in 'clear and unambiguous language'.

4. The courts will lift the veil in cases involving national security, particularly in times of war.

5. The veil has been lifted in cases where it has been shown that the corporate form was being used as a facade in order to avoid liability or to gain a benefit for the shareholders:

   a) evasion of liability to pay tax (*Commissioners of Inland Revenue v Land Securities Investment Trust Ltd*) (1969); *Littlewoods Mail Order Stores Ltd v Inland Revenue Commissioners* (1969));

   b) evasion of restraint of trade clause in contract of employment (*Gilford Motors v Horne*) attempt to avoid order of specific performance (*Jones v Lipman*).

6. It was held in *Salomon v Salomon* that the company is not the agent of the shareholders. However, the agency argument has been used in a number of cases involving groups of companies.

   a) Every company in a group is recognised as a separate legal person, and it has been argued that a subsidiary is in certain circumstances the agent of the holding company.

   b) The agency argument reinforces the principle of separate legal personality, but the issue is usually whether an agency can be inferred.

   c) In *FG Films* the court inferred agency in a case where a UK company was set up in order to acquire film distribution rights in the UK for an American holding company.

   d) In *Smith, Stone & Knight v Birmingham Corporation* the court laid down guidelines to establish whether agency could be implied between a holding company and its subsidiaries. This case has been much criticised and has not been followed.

   e) In *JH Rayner (Mincing Lane) Ltd v Department of Trade
      and Industry* (1989) – agency cannot be inferred from the
      mere fact that the company is controlled by its shareholders.
7. The high water mark of the courts' willingness to lift veils was
   DHN Ltd v London Borough of Tower Hamlets, in which it was
   held that a group of companies was a single economic unit,
   thus enabling the group to claim compensation on the
   compulsory purchase of the land even though the land from
   which the business was operated was owned by a subsidiary
   and the business was operated by the parent company.
8. This case was disapproved in *Woolfson v Srathclyde Regional
   Council* (1978); nor was the argument accepted in subsequent
   cases, including *Re Southard & Co Ltd* (1979), and *Adams v
   Cape Industries.*

2.5.2 Current position

1. In *Adams v Cape Industries* the Court of Appeal reviewed
   three of the arguments for lifting the veil discussed above: the
   agency argument, the single economic unit argument and the
   'facade' argument, and held that none applied on the facts.
2. The case signals a shift towards the view that in the absence of
   fraud, incorporators can rely on the principle of corporate
   personality.
3. This view has been affirmed in *Ord v Bellhaven Pubs Ltd*
   (1998) and *Williams v Natural Health Foods Ltd* (1998).
4. The current situation can be summarised as follows:
   a) Although agency cannot be inferred, effect will be given to
      an express agency agreement between a company and its
      members or between companies in a group. An express
      agency affirms the principle of separate personality.
   b) Following *Adams v Cape Industries,* it seems that the only
      circumstances in which the courts are likely to lift the veil
      are now:
      ● when the court is construing a statute, contract or other
        document which requires the veil to be lifted;

- when the court is satisfied that the company is a 'mere facade', so that there is an abuse of the corporate form;
- when it can be established that the company is an authorised agent of its controllers or its members, corporate or human.

2.5.3 Statutory examples

There are a number of statutory provisions which have the effect of lifting the veil, making directors or members liable for the debts of the company in certain circumstances.

ss213, 214 Insolvency Act 1985	Fraudulent and wrongful trading
s15 Company Directors Disqualification Act 1986	Person involved in management of a company in contravention of disqualification order
s24 Companies Act 1985	Reduction of number of members of public company
s349(4) Companies Act 1985	Misdescription of company on bill of exchange, promissory note, cheque, etc
schedule 9, part II Companies Act 1985	Consolidated accounts for groups of companies

2.6 CORPORATE LIABILITY

The fact that a company is an artificial person raises questions as to the limits of corporate liability.

2.6.1 Liability in contract

Liability for contracts and other commercial transactions undertaken by companies is governed by the company's objects clause in the memorandum of association and s35 of the Companies Act 1985, and the law of agency and 35A (see chapter 4).

2.6.2 Liability in tort

In tort, the concept of vicarious liability conveniently gets around the problem of imposing liability on an artificial person, as a company may be held vicariously liable for the wrongful acts of its officers and employees as long as they were acting in the course of their employment.

2.6.3 Liability for crime

1. There are clearly certain crimes which it is impossible for a company to commit since the *actus reus* could not be committed by an artificial person, for example *driving* a vehicle in an unsafe condition (*Richmond-on-Thames BC v Pinn & Wheeler Ltd* (1989)).
2. In recent years the debate has centred on whether an artificial person is able to form the necessary *mens rea* for the offence in question. In three cases in 1944 companies were convicted of offences requiring *mens rea.* (*DPP v Kent & Sussex Contracters, R v ICR Haulage Ltd, Moore v Bresler*). The principle was recognised by the House of Lords in *Tesco Supermarkets Ltd v Nattrass* (1972).
3. Following the capsizing of the Herald of Free Enterprise, the question of whether a company could be convicted of manslaughter was considered in *R v P&O European Ferries (Dover) Ltd.* It was held that it was possible for a company to commit manslaughter, as long as it could be established that a person who could be identified as the 'mind and will of the company' had the requisite *mens rea,* although in that case the company was acquitted.
4. The first successful prosecution of a company for manslaughter was *R v Kite* (1966), in which the company was fined £50,000 on conviction. The managing director of the company was also convicted and was sentenced to three years imprisonment, reduced by the Court of Appeal to two years. In this case, unlike *P & O European Ferries,* the company was

a small company, controlled by the managing director whose mental state could be attributed to the company.

5. Some of the difficulties are highlighted in *Attorney General's Reference (No 2 of 1999)* in which the trial judge directed the acquittal of Great Western Trains Ltd following a rail accident which caused the death of seven people. It had not been possible to prove *mens rea* in respect of any individual who could be identified with the company.

2.6.4 Reform

In March 1996, the Law Commission published a report *Legislating the Criminal Code: Involuntary Manslaughter* (Law Com No 237), in which the Commission recommends that:

- there should be a special offence of corporate killing, broadly corresponding to the proposed individual offence of killing by gross carelessness;
- the corporate offence should be committed only where the defendant's conduct in causing the death falls below what could reasonably be expected;
- unlike the individual offence, the corporate offence should not require the risk to be obvious, or that the defendant should be capable of appreciating the risk, thus removing some of the current difficulties associated with attributing *mens rea* to artificial persons;
- for the purposes of the corporate offence, a death should be regarded as having been caused by the conduct of a corporation if it is caused by failure, in the way in which the corporation's activities are managed or organised, to ensure the health and safety of persons employed in or affected by those activities.

CHAPTER 3
THE ARTICLES OF ASSOCIATION

The Companies Act 1985, s.1 requires that every company must have a memorandum of association. A company is also required to have articles of association, but may adopt Table A and if articles are not registered, then Table A will automatically apply. The memorandum and articles are often described as the constitution of the company, the former dealing with the company's relations with the external world and the latter with the internal regulation of the company (see Chapter 1).

3.1 CONTENT OF ARTICLES OF ASSOCIATION

A company may adopt all or part of Table A, which is a useful guide to the kind of matters contained in the articles:
- Articles 2–35 Shares
- Articles 36–63 General meetings
- Articles 64–101 Directors and company secretary
- Articles 102–110 Dividends, accounts, capitalisation of profit
- Articles 111–116 Notices of meetings

3.2 ALTERATION OF ARTICLES

1. A company may alter its articles by:
   - special resolution [s9 CA 1985];
   - agreement by all members (without a resolution) (*Cane v Jones* (1980)).
2. There are a number of rules which regulate a company's power to alter its articles, summarised in *Peter's American Delicacy Co Ltd v Heath* (Australian HC 1939). Note in particular:

a) A company's power to alter its articles may be restricted by the memorandum, since any provision in the articles which conflicts with the memorandum will be invalid unless the provision in question could lawfully have been contained in the articles and the memorandum does not prohibit its alteration: *Allen v Gold Reefs of West Africa Ltd* (1900).

b) The power to alter articles must be exercised bona fide for the benefit of the company as a whole : *Allen v Gold Reefs of West Africa Ltd.*

c) A member cannot challenge an alteration which was carried out bona fide for the benefit of the company as a whole, even if such alteration has affected the member's personal rights as long as the altered article was intended to apply indiscriminately to all members (*Greenhalgh v Arderne Cinemas Ltd* (1951)).

d) The court will generally accept the majority's bona fide view of what is for the benefit of the company as a whole, as long as the alteration is not one which no reasonable person could consider to be for the benefit of the company.

3.2.1 Statutory restrictions on power to alter articles

- S16: a member is not bound by a change which requires him/her to take more shares or in any way increase the member's liability, without the written agreement of the member.
- SS125–127: any alteration which varies class rights must follow the procedures laid down in these sections (see chapter 6).
- SS380, 80(8): any alteration must be notified to the Registrar within 15 days of the alteration.

3.3 CONTRACTUAL EFFECT OF MEMORANDUM AND ARTICLES OF ASSOCIATION

1. The ownership of shares in a company gives rise to certain rights and obligations. A company is an artificial person in its own right as well as an association of its members, and is therefore able to contract with its members.
2. This is recognised and reinforced in s14 of the Companies Act, which provides that subject to provisions in the Act itself, the memorandum and articles of association operate as if they had been signed and sealed by each member.
3. Although s14 does not explicitly describe the relationship as contractual, the section is interpreted as creating a contract between the company and its members and the members *inter se*.
4. S14 refers to both the memorandum and articles of association, but discussion of the s14 contract tends to focus on the articles since this contains the rules for internal management of the company.

3.3.1 Special features of the section 14 contract

Ordinary contract	s14 contract
Terms agreed by parties	Member usually accepts terms by purchase of shares in company
Terms provide for obligations/rights which when performed come to an end	Memorandum and articles create ongoing rights/obligations as company's constitution
Terms only altered by agreement of parties	Memorandum (objects) (s4, CA 1985) and articles (s9 CA 1985) can be altered by special resolution (75% of members)
Rectification available	Rectification not available (*Scott v Scott* (1940))
Damages usual remedy for breach	Damages usually not appropriate (but may be claimed for liquidated sum, e.g. dividend); declaration usual remedy

3.3.2 The scope of s14

1. The scope of the s14 contract has been considered in a number of cases, which cannot easily be reconciled. The following points are clearly established:

   a) Once registered, the memorandum and articles constitute a contract between the members and the company and between the members *inter se* (*Wood v Odessa Waterworks Co* (1889)). This contract gives rise to:

      - contractual rights against the company (*Hickman v Kent & Romney Marsh Sheep-Breeders Association* (1915));
      - contractual rights for shareholders against fellow shareholders (*Rayfield v Hands* (1960)).

   b) A claim based on s14 made by an **outsider** (that is, a person making a claim in a capacity other than that of a member) will not succeed (*Eley v Positive Government Security Life Assurance* (1876); *Beattie v E and F Beattie* (1938). It should be noted here that 'outsider' has been very strictly defined, so that a person claiming as a director, even if s/he is also a member, will fail.

3.3.3 Cases giving guidance

1. The following rights contained in the articles may be enforced by members:

   - provision in the articles requiring directors to purchase shares from member wishing to leave company (*Rayfield v Hands*);
   - right to exercise vote at general meeting (*Pender v Lushington* (1877))
   - payment of dividend, duly declared;
   - right to bring proceedings to restrain an act which is outside the capacity of the company (s35(2) CA 1985) or the powers of the directors (s35A(4) CA 1985);
   - right to enforce veto on certain acts by directors (*Salmon v Quin & Axtens* (1909)).

2. The company may enforce any provision in the articles requiring that a dispute between it and its members be referred to arbitration (*Hickman v Kent and Romney Marsh Sheepbreeders Association* (1915)).

3.3.4 Enforcing 'outsider rights'

1. It is less clear whether 'outsider' rights can be enforced by a person bringing a claim as a member, on the basis that every member has the right to have the company's business conducted in accordance with the articles.
2. This was suggested by K.W. Wedderburn in an important article in 1957 and has been the subject of academic debate.
3. It is suggested that if the provision in the articles relates to a constitutional matter, for example those listed above then a member will be able to enforce the article as a contract.
4. But if the matter relates to an aspect of internal organisation or management of the company, for example the right to be paid a salary or the right to be the company's solicitor (*Eley v Positive Life)* then the provision will not be enforceable.

3.4 DIRECTORS, THE ARTICLES AND EXTRINSIC CONTRACTS

1. Directors may or may not also be members of their companies.
2. In their capacity as directors they have no contractual relationship with the company under s14.
3. However, the company can make contracts with its directors and other third parties, which expressly or impliedly incorporate terms contained in the articles, for example articles about directors' remuneration, may be incorporated in a contract of service.
4. Where an article provides for the employment of a director, but there is no contract, the court may imply an extrinsic contract (*Re New British Iron Co ex p. Beckwith* (1898)).

5. These rights can be enforced against the company without relying on the articles, but alteration of the articles may vary the terms of the contract.

6. The articles can be altered at any time by special resolution, thus varying the terms of the contract, but terms cannot be altered retrospectively (*Swabey v Port Darwin Gold Mining Co* (1889)).

7. If provisions from the articles are incorporated into extrinsic contracts, alteration of the articles may result in breach of the extrinsic contract. A third party cannot prevent alteration of the articles, but in such cases the company may be liable to pay damages.

3.5 REFORM

1. When Australian company law was revised in 1985, the wording of the equivalent section (which used to be the same as s14) was changed to state explicitly that the memorandum and articles have effect as a contract between the company and each member and between each member and every other member.

2. This was considered by the Law Commission in its report *Shareholder Remedies* but no change to current British legislation was considered necessary.

3. However, the Company Law Steering Group considered that s14 'is so misleading' that it would be desirable to:
   - lay down a statutory provision explaining the extent to which individual shareholders are entitled to enforce the constitution;
   - abolish the contractual character of the rights.

Does the company have
the capacity to make the
Contract?
  – Objects clause
  – S35

Is the Contract
binding
on the company?

Does the person purporting to act for
the company have the authority?
  – S35(A)
  – General law of agency
  – Rule in Turquand's case

4.1 THE *ULTRA VIRES* DOCTINE: HISTORICAL PERSPECTIVE

4.1.1 The contractual capacity of companies

1. Every company must have a memorandum of association: sections 1 and 2 CA 1985. Since 1856 successive Companies Acts have required that an objects clause be included in the memorandum of association (see chapter 1).
2. The objects clause sets out the activities for which the company was formed and any activity outside this statement of objects is said to be *ultra vires* (outside the company's capacity) and at common law any such transaction was void.
3. The reasons for the rule were:
   - that shareholders are entitled to know the purpose for which their investment was to be used;
   - it was supposed to protect creditors, who were deemed to know the contents of the memorandum.
4. The memorandum also commonly included a statement of the powers conferred on the company to enable it to carry out its objects. This led to confusion until the law was clarified in *Rolled Steel Products (Holdings) Ltd v British Steel Corporation* (1986).
5. The *ultra vires* rule was strengthened by the doctrine of constructive notice which provided that persons who dealt with companies were taken to know what the capacity of the company was because of the fact that the memorandum was (and is) a public document. This sometimes led to very harsh results (*Re Jon Beauforte (London) Ltd* (1953)).

4.1.2 Development of the law

1. In *Ashbury Railway Carriage & Iron Co Ltd v Riche (1875)* the House of Lords held that a company did not have the capacity to enter into a contract outside the objects clause and therefore such a contract could not be enforced by either party.

2. The difficulties were explored in subsequent cases and ingenious draftsmen found ways around the restrictive approach of the courts.

3. It became commonplace for companies to include long objects clauses with a number of separate clauses followed by a clause to the effect that each and every paragraph contained a separate object of the company – known as a *Cotman v Brougham* clause, since such practice was somewhat reluctantly accepted as valid in that case.

4. Another device used by companies was the 'subjective' objects clause, considered by the court in *Bell Houses v City Wall Properties Ltd (1966)*. Two main objects were followed by a clause stating that the company had capacity 'to carry on any other trade or business whatsoever which can, in the opinion of the board of directors, be advantageously carried on by the company in connection with or as ancillary to any of the above businesses or the general business of the company.'

4.1.3 The need for reform

1. The *ultra vires* rule has been the subject of controversy over a long period. The difficulty arises because the company is owned by its members, and yet it is the directors, who may not necessarily be members themselves, who conduct the company's business.

2. This leads to a tension between the need to ensure that the company's property is used for the benefit of the members, and the need not to place undue constraints on the directors' freedom to take the company forward.

3. The objects clause and the *ultra vires* doctrine achieved the former at common law, but not the latter.

4. Further, application of the *ultra vires* doctrine allowed companies to avoid transactions, producing harsh results for third parties.

5. In *Cotman v Brougham* (1918) Lord Parker said, 'The narrower the objects expressed in the memorandum, the less is the subscribers' risk, but the wider such objects, the greater the security of those who transact business with the company.'

4.1.4 Proposals for reform

1. 1945 – the Cohen Committee (Cmd 6659) recommended that a company should have the same powers as an individual as regards third parties.
2. 1962 – the Jenkins Committee (Cmnd 1749) recommended the abolition of the constructive notice rule, but did not favour full abolition of the *ultra vires* doctrine itself.
3. No change was made until 1973, when the UK's entry into the EEC made it necessary to comply with Article 9 of the First Company Law Directive, and s9(1) of the European Communities Act 1972 (consolidated as s35 Companies Act 1985) provided:
'In favour of a person dealing with a company in good faith, any transaction decided on by the directors shall be deemed to be one which it is within the capacity of the company to enter into, and the power of the directors to bind the company shall be deemed to be free of any limitation under the memorandum or articles of association; ...'
This provision gave rise to considerable uncertainty and the drive for reform continued.
4. 1986 – The Prentice Report recommended that companies should have capacity to do any act whatsoever and should have the option of not stating their objects in their memorandum of association.

4.2 STATUTORY REFORM OF *ULTRA VIRES*

1. In 1989, s35 of the Companies Act 1985 was re-enacted and now provides that:
   - the validity of an act done by a company shall not be called into question on the ground of lack of capacity by reason of anything in the company's memorandum (s35(1));

- *but* a member can bring proceedings to stop the doing of an act which would be beyond the company's capacity but for s35(1) *unless* the company is under a legal obligation to do the act (s35(2));
- directors have a duty to act within their powers as set out in the memorandum;
- members can ratify an *ultra vires* act by **special resolution**;
- a **separate special resolution** is required to absolve the directors from liability arising from their breach of duty (s35(3)).

2. While this section effectively abolishes the rule as far as transactions between the company and third parties are concerned, the objects clause and the *ultra vires* doctrine may still have application with respect to the internal management of the company.

3. The 1989 Act also inserted s3A which allows companies to state that their object is 'to carry on business as a general commercial company'.

4. Professor Sealy comments '[This] can be seen as a well-meaning attempt to encourage the draftsmen of company memoranda to abandon the traditional long-winded objects clause ... It appears, however, that the draftsmen have not taken the bait. Many have sought to have the best of both worlds, by continuing their use of lengthy precedents and adding a further clause listing the carrying on of business as a general commercial company as an additional object!'

4.2.1 Reform

1. The Company Law Steering Group recommends the replacement of s35 with a statement that a company has unlimited contractual capacity.

2. This is reflected in clause 1(5) of the draft Companies Bill, which provides in clause 1(5) that company formed under this Act has unlimited capacity.

3. It follows that it is recommended that s3A Companies Act 1985 be abolished.

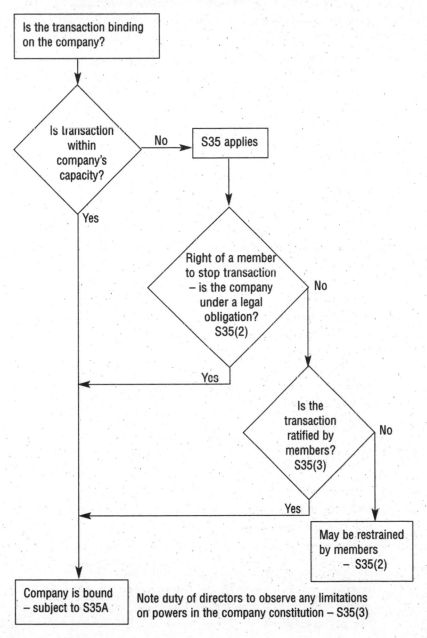

4.3 AGENCY PRINCIPLES AND COMPANY LAW

1. Separate legal personality ensures that a company can contract with third parties, but being an artificial person, a company can only contract through agents.
2. In relation to transactions with third parties, it is necessary to distinguish between the capacity of a company and the authority of the directors and other agents to deal on behalf of the company.
3. The issue here is whether the board of directors, an individual director or some other person can commit the company to a binding contract.

4.3.1 The board of directors

1. The directors of a company have actual authority to bind the company if they are acting for the purpose of attaining the company's objects (*Rolled Steel Products (Holdings) Ltd v British Steel Corporation*).
2. Articles of association usually provide that the company's business shall be managed by the board of directors (art.70, Table A) so all powers of management are delegated to the board. In this way the company appoints its agents and gives them authority.
3. The directors, acting as a board, are agents of the company and a third party can usually rely on the actions of the directors in accordance with the ordinary principles of the law of agency.

4.4 STATUTORY PROVISIONS: S35A CA 1985

1. S35 provides that in certain instances the power of the directors may be limited by the company's constitution, for example the general meeting may have the right to veto the sale of certain assets.

2. S35A deals with the authority of directors to bind the company and, like s35, it is intended to increase the security of third parties dealing with a company.

3. S35A provides that in favour of a person dealing with a company in good faith, the power of the board of directors to bind the company or authorise others to do so, shall be deemed to be free of any limitation under the company's constitution.

4. 'Dealing' covers any transaction or act to which the company is a party (s35A(2)(a)).

5. A person is not to be regarded as acting in bad faith just because he or she was aware that the transaction was beyond the authority of the directors (s35A(2)(b)).

6. A person is presumed to have acted in good faith unless the contrary is proved (s35A(2)c)).

7. A member can bring proceedings to stop an act which is beyond the powers of the directors, but:
   - not if the act has given rise to legal obligations (s3A(4));
   - the section does not affect any liability incurred by the directors, or other person, as a result of exceeding their powers (s35A(5));
   - a person dealing with a company is not bound to enquire whether the power of the board of directors is limited by the constitution (s35B).

4.4.1 Modification of s35A

UNIVERSITY OF BRISTOL LIBRARY ENGINEERING

1. S322A modifies s35A and restricts the protection given to third parties dealing with a company.

2. When the parties to the transaction include:
   - a director of the company or its holding company;
   - a person connected with such a director;
   - a person connected with a company with whom such a director is associated;
   - the transaction is voidable by the company and the person concerned is liable to account to the company for any profit and to indemnify the company for any loss arising from the contract.

SECTION 35A

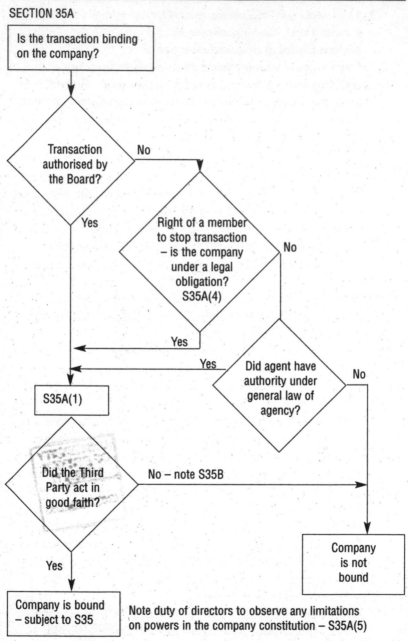

Is the transaction binding on the company?

Transaction authorised by the Board?

No

Yes

Right of a member to stop transaction – is the company under a legal obligation? S35A(4)

No

Yes

Yes

Did agent have authority under general law of agency?

No

S35A(1)

Did the Third Party act in good faith?

No – note S35B

Company is not bound

Yes

Company is bound – subject to S35

Note duty of directors to observe any limitations on powers in the company constitution – S35A(5)

3. The transaction will not be voidable if:
- restitution is no longer possible;
- the company is indemnified for any loss;
- rights acquired bona fide for value and without notice of the directors exceeding their powers would be affected;
- the transaction is ratified by the company in general meeting.

4.5 OTHER AGENTS

1. Under s35A the authority of the board to bind the company, or to authorise others to do so cannot be called into question.

2. Thus the board may delegate authority to others, for example a single director or an employee of the company. But in order to decide whether the board has in fact given authority to another person will involve application of the general law of agency.

3. In the law of agency, an agent will only be able to make a contract which binds the principal if the agent is acting with the **authority** of the principal.

4. Authority may be either **actual** or **ostensible**:

a) Actual authority
- *express:* authority expressly given to the agent by the principal;
- *implied:* authority implied by virtue of the fact that it is necessary to enable the agent to exercise the authority expressly given (*Hely Hutchinson v Brayhead Ltd* (1967)).

b) Ostensible (or apparent) authority: the authority which the agent appears to have by virtue of a representation made by the principal: *Freeman & Lockyer v Buckhurst Properties (Mangal) Ltd (1964); Armagas Ltd v Mundogas SA* (1986). Ostensible authority may be conferred by a particular job title (*Panorama Developments v Fidelis Furnishing Fabrics* (1971)).

5. Ostensible authority depends upon:
- representation to the third party;
- representation made by the principal or by persons who had actual authority; an agent cannot represent himself as

having authority (*Armagas v Mundogas* (1986));
- reliance by third party on the representation (previously) that the company had capacity to enter into the contract (no longer relevant by virtue of s35).

4.6 THE INDOOR MANAGEMENT RULE

1. The application of agency rules has always caused some difficulties in company law, particularly in the context of limitations on authority of directors imposed by the company's constitution.
2. The doctrine of constructive notice exacerbated the problem, since anyone dealing with a company was deemed to know the contents of the memorandum and articles of association, whether or not he or she had actually seen these documents.

4.6.1 The rule in Turquand's case

1. The rule in *Turquand's case* (the indoor management rule), developed alongside the doctrine of constructive notice and mitigates its effect.
2. Where:
   - the directors have power to bind the company, but certain preliminaries must be gone through, and
   - there are no suspicious circumstances
   a person dealing with a company is entitled to assume that all matters of internal procedure have been complied with (*Royal British Bank v Turquand* (1876); *Mahoney v East Holyford Mining Company* (1875); *Rolled Steel Products (Holdings) Ltd v British Steel Corporation* (1982)).

4.6.2 Is the rule in Turquand's case still relevant?

1. Section 35A is wider than the rule in *Turquand's case* since knowledge of a defect prevents the third party from relying on *Turquand* (*Morris v Kanssen* (1946)), while knowledge of limitations on directors' powers does not stop a third party from relying on s35A (s35B). The introduction of s35A has largely subsumed the rule in *Turquand's case*.
2. However, the rule may still have application where the limitation on the board's power to act is not strictly constitutional, such as when a decision to enter into a transaction is made by an inquorate board.

4.7 ALTERATION OF THE MEMORANDUM OF ASSOCIATION

1. A company may alter its memorandum with respect to the objects clause (s4 CA 1985).
2. However, a shareholder may apply to the court for the alteration to be cancelled.
3. If an application is made, the alteration is ineffective unless confirmed by the court.

CHAPTER 5

THE GENERAL MEETING

5.1 INTRODUCTION

Types of meeting
Class meeting
General meeting
Annual General
meeting (AGM)
Extraordinary
General meeting
(EGM)

MEETINGS

Voting
Usually by a show of
hands with each member
having one vote
A **poll** may be
demanded – each
member has a vote for
every share held
A **proxy** can vote on a
poll but not on a show
of hands

Resolutions
Decision made at meetings
Can be:
- ordinary resolutions
  (51% of vote)
- special resolutions
  (75% of vote and notice)
- extraordinary resolutions
  (75% of vote)
- written resolutions (s390(4))
- elective resolutions (s379A)

1. A company is both an association of its members (who are the
   owners of the company) and a person in its own right.

2. The Act provides that a company must have:
- members: ss22–4 (private company: minimum one; plc: minimum 2);
- directors: s282 (private company: minimum one; plc: minimum two);
- a secretary: s283.

3. But a company is an artificial person and therefore able to act only through its agents. A company appoints its agents through the mechanism of the general meeting.

4. Further, a formal mechanism for exchanging information and making certain important decisions is needed, and, under the Companies Act 1985, the meeting is the focus of corporate decision-making by the shareholders and accountability on the part of the directors.

5.2 WHAT IS A MEETING?

1. General definitions:

1. Class meeting	Open to members of a particular class of shareholders or creditors (see chapters 6 and 12)
2. General meeting	Open to all members – may be AGM or EGM
3. Annual general meeting	a) Must be held within 18 months after incorporation and then in each calendar year with not more than 15 months between meetings. If directors do not call AGM, a member may require the Secretary of State to do so (s366).
	b) Private companies can elect to dispense with holding AGM (s366A)
	c) Purpose of AGM – to consider accounts and reports of auditors and directors; to declare dividend; to elect directors and auditors.
4. Extraordinary general meeting	a) Any meeting which is not an AGM is an EGM.
	b) Under Table A only directors can usually call an EGM, but under s368 members who between hold 10% of company's voting shares may deliver a requisition demanding that directors call a meeting.
	c) The court may call a meeting under s371.

2. At common law, one person cannot constitute a meeting: *Sharp v Dawes* (1876)

3. But there are exceptions:
- class meetings where there is only one member of the class;
- private companies which have only one member;
- under s367 CA 1985 the Secretary of State for Trade & Industry can direct that a meeting be held and fix the quorum at one (*Re Sticky Fingers Restaurant Ltd* (1992)).

4. A meeting can be held by telephone (*Re Associated Color laboratories Ltd* (1970).

5. A meeting can be held in different rooms with audio-visual links between them (*Byng v London life Association Ltd.* (1990).

5.3 REFORM

1. The AGM is recognised as an unsatisfactory forum for the exchange of views and the making of decisions in modern companies, especially large public companies with both small private investors and institutional shareholders. The Company Law Review Steering Group made a number of radical proposals including the abolition of the AGM, but this didn't gain wide support in the consultation.

2. In the *Final Report* the Steering Group recommends:
- 'that public companies should be enabled to dispense with the holding of AGMs, provided the members unanimously so decide';
- private companies should be able to dispense with the need to hold AGMs by special resolution;
- new private companies, unless they opt into the AGM regime should be free of any obligation to hold them.

5.4 VOTING

1. Generally voting at general meetings is by **show of hands** with each member having one vote. A **poll** may be demanded in accordance with the statute and the articles, in which case a written record is kept and each member has a vote for every share held. Table A article 54 allows a poll to be demanded by two members. S373 (1) lays down detailed minimum requirements as to who may demand a poll at general meetings.

2. A member who cannot attend a meeting can appoint a **proxy** to attend and the proxy has a right to vote on a poll, but not on a show of hands. Detailed provisions with respect to proxies are to be found in Table A, articles 60ff.

3. Reform: The Company Law Steering Group recommended that:
   - public companies should allow proxies to speak;
   - proxies should be allowed to vote on a show of hands.

4. S375 allows a corporate member to appoint a human representative with the same powers as an individual member.

5.5 RESOLUTIONS

1. Decisions made at meetings are expressed in resolutions:

2. There are the following types of resolution:
   - ordinary resolution – 51% of vote;
   - special resolution – 75% of vote; 21 days notice of intention to propose required;
   - extraordinary resolution – 75% of vote; no notice required;
   - written resolution – agreed by all members entitled to vote; s380(4);
   - elective resolutions (s379A) – apply only to private companies and are not effective unless adopted at a meeting of which at least 21 days notice of intention to propose has been given.

3. Reform: Company law review steering group propose the abolition of extraordinary resolutions. The requirement for an extraordinary resolution should be replaced with a special resolution.

5.5.1 Ordinary resolutions

1. Unless otherwise stipulated in the Companies Act or in the company's constitution, company decisions can be taken by ordinary resolution.

2. Note in particular that an ordinary resolution is required to:
- approve market purchase by company of its own shares (s166(1));
- remove directors (s303);
- approve compensation to directors for loss of office (s313 (1)).

5.5.2 Special resolutions

1. A special resolution is required for the following purposes, according the the Companies Act 1985:
- to change objects of company (s4);
- to alter articles of association (s9(1));
- to change company's name (s28(1));
- to ratify transaction outside objects clause (s35(3));
- to relieve directors of liability for transaction outside objects (s35(3));
- to allow private company to re-register as public company (s43(1));
- to allow public company to re-register as private company (s53(1));
- to reduce share capital if authorised by articles (s135(1))
- to approve financial assistance for acquisition of shares in company (s155(4),(5));
- to approve payment of capital for redemption of purchase of company's own shares (s173(2));
- to approve directors' service contracts for periods of more than 5 years (s319(3));
- to approve substantial property transactions (s320(1)).

2. The Insolvency Act 1986 requires a special resolution:
- to resolve that the company should be wound up voluntarily (s84(1));
- in voluntary liquidation, to approve transfer of shares to another company (s110);
- to resolve to petition for compulsory winding up (s122(1)(a)).

3. Note:
- the list above is not exhaustive;
- the company's memorandum or articles may require a special resolution for certain decisions.

5.5.3 Dissentient members

1. In certain circumstances dissentient members have a right to apply to the court to have a resolution set aside:
- alteration of objects clause (s5);
- alteration of condition in memorandum which could have been in articles (s17);
- registration of public company as private company (s54)
- alteration of class right (s127);
- private company providing financial assistance for purchase of own shares (s157);
- private company making payment out of capital (s176).

5.5.4 Remedies

1. Confirm or cancel resolution (s127).
2. Others: such relief as is just and equitable.

5.5.5 Elective resolutions

1. An elective resolution is required for a private company to elect to adopt any of the following provisions of the CA 1985:
- variation of duration of authority to allot shares (s80A);
- dispensing with laying of accounts and reports before general meeting (s252);
- a dispensing with holding of AGM (s366);
- majority required to authorise short notice of meeting (s369(4));
- dispensing with annual appointment of auditors (s386).

CHAPTER 6

CAPITAL

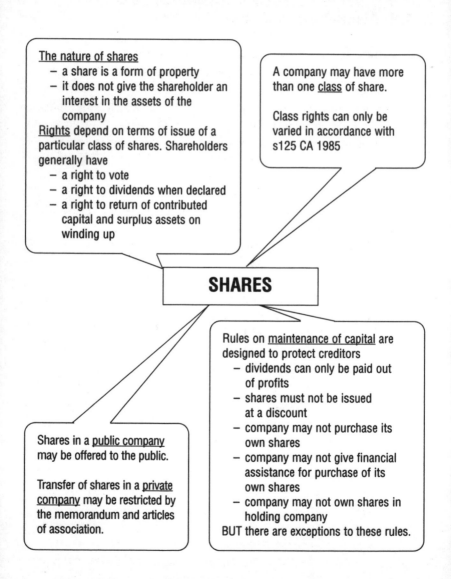

The nature of shares
- a share is a form of property
- it does not give the shareholder an interest in the assets of the company

Rights depend on terms of issue of a particular class of shares. Shareholders generally have
- a right to vote
- a right to dividends when declared
- a right to return of contributed capital and surplus assets on winding up

A company may have more than one class of share.

Class rights can only be varied in accordance with s125 CA 1985

SHARES

Rules on maintenance of capital are designed to protect creditors
- dividends can only be paid out of profits
- shares must not be issued at a discount
- company may not purchase its own shares
- company may not give financial assistance for purchase of its own shares
- company may not own shares in holding company

BUT there are exceptions to these rules.

Shares in a public company may be offered to the public.

Transfer of shares in a private company may be restricted by the memorandum and articles of association.

6.1 THE NATURE OF SHARES

1. The issue of shares is one way in which a company raises capital.
2. Shareholders undertake to contribute an agreed amount of capital to the company and this is then the limit of the shareholder's liability.
3. A share is a way of measuring each member's interest in the company. So if a company has an authorised and issued share capital of £10,000 divided into £1 shares and shareholder A owns 1000 shares, he or she owns 10% of the company and will, on a poll, command 10% of the vote. The 'say' which each shareholder has is in proportion to the number of shares held.

6.1.1 Effects of shareholding

- Profits may be shared among shareholders by way of dividend.
- Each shareholder usually has the right to vote.
- If the company is wound up when not insolvent, capital may be returned to members.
- Shares in a plc may be offered to the public.
- Shares in a private company may be transferred in accordance with the memorandum and articles.

6.1.2 Share capital

1. *Authorised share capital* (nominal share capital): the total nominal value of shares that may be allotted to members in accordance with the memorandum of association. There is no correlation between the nominal value of shares and the market value. The authorised share capital can be increased by ordinary resolution (s121 CA 1985).
2. *Issued share capital*: the proportion of the authorised share capital that has actually been issued to shareholders.
3. *Paid up share capital*: the amount actually contributed to the share capital of the company, excluding any premium and excluding calls made but not yet paid. If partly paid shares are

issued, the shareholder will pay part of the price when the shares are issued and will be liable to pay the remainder at some time in the future.

4. *Uncalled capital:* the amount still owed.

6.1.3 Reform

The Company Law Review Steering Group *Final Report* proposes the abolition of the concept of authorised share capital. The constitutional document of the company would contain a statement of the share capital allotted to members on formation of the company.

6.1.4 Types of shares

1. *Ordinary shares:* Art.54, Table A provides that each member shall have one vote on a show of hands and one vote per share on a poll. The dividend is that recommended by the directors, and the amount payable on a distribution of assets on a winding up is proportional to the nominal value of the shares.

2. *Preference shares:* Usually entitles the holders to a dividend of a fixed amount per share to be paid in priority to other shareholders. These may be:
   - cumulative: if the dividend is not paid in one year, then the shareholder will be entitled to double the following year, and so on;
   - non-cumulative: the dividend will lapse if the company is unable to pay it in any one year.

3. *Deferred shares:* Now rare. Promoters used to take shares which would not qualify for a dividend until the ordinary shareholders had received one.

4. *Redeemable shares:* Shares that are issued with a provision that they may be bought back by the company at a later date, at the option of either the company or the shareholder.

5. *Non-voting shares:* Similar rights to ordinary shareholders, but no right to vote.

6.2 ALLOTMENT OF SHARES

6.2.1 Issue and allotment

1. Directors may not allot shares (except in specified circumstances) unless they have authority to do so either by the articles or by ordinary resolution (s80 CA 1985). A public company cannot give authority to allot shares for more than five years.
2. Shares may be issued in exchange for cash or for other forms of property, for example in a takeover the offeror company may offer its shares in return for shares in the offeree company.
3. Shares are allotted when a person acquires the unconditional right to be entered in the register of members in respect of that share (s738(1)).
4. Shares are issued when the holder's name is entered in the register of members (*Re Heaton's Steel and Iron Co, Blythe's Case* (1876); *National Westminster Bank plc v Inland Revenue Commissioners* (1995)).
5. A company may alter its share capital in accordance with s121 CA 1985 if allowed by the company's articles of association.

6.2.2 Pre-emption rights

1. A member's influence within a company depends upon the proportion of shares held.
2. In order to ensure that this influence is not diluted, s89 provides that before any equity shares are allotted in exchange for a cash contribution, they should first be offered to existing shareholders.
3. However, a private company may include a provision in its memorandum or articles of association that an issue of shares may be made without offering to existing members (s91 CA 1985).

6.2.3 Offering shares to the public

1. Only a plc may offer its shares to the public. Under s81 CA 1985, a private company commits an offence if it offers shares to the public.
2. Of some 1.2 million registered companies in the UK, only about 2000 are listed by the UK Listing Authority. Under the Financial Services and Markets Act 2000, the Financial Services Authority is designated as the UK Listing Authority (UKLA).
3. The UKLA maintains an Official List of securities which are deemed suitable for trading on stock exchanges and which are admitted to trading on at least one Recognised Investment Exchange (RIE).

6.2.4 The prospectus

1. Under the Listing Particulars Directive (80/390 EEC) a company requiring listing must submit a Listing Particulars, which is a public document, to the UKLA.
2. Under Directive 89/298/EEC, implemented in the UK by the Public Offer of Securities Regulations 1995, a prospectus must be made available to investors when a company (whether listed or not) proposes to offer shares to the public for the first time.
3. The contents of the prospectus are laid down in the Listing Rules.
4. In general, the prospectus must disclose all the information which investors and their professional advisers would reasonably need in order to make an informed decision whether to invest.

6.2.5 Misleading statements and omissions in listing particulars and prospectus

1. Remedies are available to people induced to subscribe for shares by misleading or untrue statements under:

- the common law;
- Misrepresentation Act 1967;
- Financial Services and Markets Act 2000 s90, Schedule 10.
2. It is a criminal offence to give false or misleading information in connection with an application for a listing offer of shares to the public.

6.3 LOAN CAPITAL: DEBENTURES AND REGISTRATION OF CHARGES

6.3.1 A company can also raise capital by borrowing, often by way of debenture. A debenture is a document evidencing a loan.
1. There are significant differences between shares and debentures:
   - shares create rights of membership, for example the right to attend general meetings and vote, a debenture holder is a creditor of the company, whose rights are fixed by contract;
   - a shareholder is entitled to a dividend if one is declared, a debenture holder is entitled to payment of interest.
2. A debenture may be secured or unsecured. Security may be by means of a fixed or floating charge:
   - a fixed charge may be created over certain company property such as buildings;
   - a floating charge may be created over fluctuating assets, allowing the company to deal with the property until crystallisation (*Re Yorkshire Woolcombers Association Ltd* (1903)).
3. A floating charge crystallises when:
   - the company no longer carries on business;
   - the security is enforced by virtue of a clause in the debenture (*Re Brightlife Ltd*) (1986)
   - the company goes into liquidation.

6.3.2 Registration of charges

1. s398 provides that a registerable charge (such charges are listed in s396) must be registered within 21 days of its creation.

2. Failure to register a charge may result in the company and its officers being fined.
3. Under s399, if a registerable charge is not registered, it will be void against an administrator or liquidator of the company (see chapter 12).

6.4 MAINTENANCE OF CAPITAL

6.4.1 General principles

1. One way in which a company raises capital to carry out its objects is by the issue of shares.
2. A member's liability on the winding up of a company is the amount which s/he has paid, or agreed to pay in the case of partly paid shares, for his or her shares.
3. The capital contribution of shareholders provides some security for the company's creditors and the law therefore lays down strict and complex rules in relation to the reduction of capital.
4. To a lawyer, the term 'nominal capital' means the sum set out in the memorandum of association.
5. This can be spent (and lost) in the course of carrying on the company's business, but it cannot be returned to members, as this would amount to a reduction of capital, with the result that creditors would have less security.
6. In the case of a company not in liquidation, payments to shareholders can only be made out of profits, usually by way of dividend.

6.4.2 The main rules relating to the maintenance of capital

Section CA 1985	Rule	Main exceptions
	A company may not reduce its capital (*Trevor v Whitworth*)	Court may sanction reduction of capital under s135, if authorised by articles
ss263–281	Distributions (dividends) may only be paid out of distributable profits	
s100	A company may not issue shares at a discount	For private companies there is no rule requiring valuation of non-cash asset.
s143	A company may not purchase its own shares	Private company has power to issue redeemable shares if authorised by articles and can redeem or purchase out of capital (ss159–162). Plc can issue redeemable shares if authorised by articles, redeemable out of distributable profits or receipts from fresh offer.
ss151–158	A company may not give financial assistance for the purchase of its own shares	Can give financial assistance if principle purpose is not merely to give such assistance and company acts in good faith. Private company can give assistance out of distributable profits (s155).
s23	A company may not own shares in its holding company	

6.4.3 Reduction of capital: the general rule

1. The general rule is that a reduction of capital is illegal unless authorised by statute (*Trevor v Whitworth* (1887)).

UNIVERSITY BRISTOL LIBRARY

ENGINEERING

2. S135 allows a company to carry out a reduction of capital if:
- it is authorised to do so in its articles (Table A, art 34 allows this);
- a special resolution is passed;
- the reduction is confirmed by the court.

6.4.4 The role of the court

1. The court's main concern in approving reductions of capital is the protection of creditors, and the legislation provides opportunities for creditors to object (ss 135–137).
2. In deciding whether to confirm a resolution for the reduction of capital the court must:
   - be assured that the interests of existing creditors are protected;
   - ensure that the procedure by which the reduction is carried out is correct (*Scottish Insurance Corporation Ltd v Wilsons & Clyde Coal Co Ltd* (1949)).
3. The court will not sanction a scheme if it is unfair. It must consider whether the scheme is fair and equitable between shareholders of different classes and between individual shareholders of the same class.
4. If the reduction of capital involves treating members of a class differently, then unless all members of the class have consented to the reduction, the procedure under ss425–7 (see later) offers better protection to minorities than the procedure under ss135–141.

6.4.5 Dividends

1. Dividends may be declared as provided in the articles.
2. Members have a right to receive a dividend once it has been declared.
3. A company shall not make a distribution except out of profits available for the purpose (s263(1)).
4. A **public** company cannot make a distribution which would result in the amount of the net assets becoming less than the

aggregate of its called-up share capital and undistributable reserves (s264).

6.4.6 Consequences of unlawful distribution

1. The directors who authorised an unlawful distribution are liable to repay the money to the company;
2. shareholders may be liable to repay an unlawful dividend (s277).

6.4.7 Issues at a discount

1. Shares can be issued at below their market value, but members must pay at least the full **nominal** value for their shares (s100 CA 1985, *Ooregum Gold Mining Co of India Ltd v Roper* (1892)).
2. If shares are paid for by a non-cash asset or assets, the rule may be difficult to enforce. In the case of private companies, there is no requirement that non-cash assets should be formally valued (*Re Wragg* (1897)).
3. S103 applies only to public companies and requires that if shares are issued for a consideration other than cash, the consideration must be valued before allotment.

6.4.8 Purchase by a company of its own shares

1. *Trevor v Whitworth* (1887) established the principle that a company may not purchase its own shares – this would amount to a reduction of capital.
2. This proved to be somewhat inconvenient, especially for private companies, and the rule has been the subject of reform and a number of exceptions have been introduced (ss143–181 CA 1985).
3. The general rule does not apply to the five exceptions set out in s143(3), and the following three are especially important:
   ● a redemption or purchase of shares in accordance with Chapter VII CA 1985;

- the acquisition of shares in a reduction of capital duly made;
- the purchase of shares in pursuance of an order of the court.

4. Ss160–162 allow a company to purchase its own shares as prescribed by the Act, as long as
   - the company is authorised to do so by its articles (Table A, art.35 gives authorisation);
   - the purchase is made out of distributable profits.

5. Private companies only may purchase their own shares out of capital, subject to safeguards for creditors (ss173–176).

6. Note: a company may not own shares in its holding company (s23 CA 1985).

6.4.9 Financial assistance for purchase of own shares

1. The general rule is that a company may not give financial assistance for the purchase of its own shares. For example it may not:
   - lend or give money to someone to buy its shares;
   - lend or give money to someone to pay back bank finance raised to buy its shares;
   - guarantee or provide security for a bank loan to finance purchase of its shares;
   - buy assets from a person at an overvalue to enable that person to purchase its shares (*Belmont Finance Corporation v Williams Furniture Ltd (No 2) (1980)*).

2. It is a criminal offence for a company or its subsidiary to give financial assistance directly or indirectly for the purchase of the company's shares (s151).

3. Exceptions are set out in s153(1). Financial assistance is not prohibited if:
   - it is given if good faith and in the interests of the company;
   - the acquisition of shares is not the principal purpose, but is 'an incidental part of some larger purpose' (*Brady v Brady (1988)*).

4. Other examples covered by s153 include:
   - financing employees' share scheme;
   - redeeming or repurchasing its shares under a properly approved scheme;
   - paying up an issue of bonus shares;
   - as part of the ordinary business of finance companies.
5. The rules are further relaxed for **Private** companies, which may give financial assistance for the purchase of their own shares if the company's net assets are not thereby reduced.

6.4.10 Remedies and sanctions

1. These are as follows:
   - a prohibited loan will be void;
   - the company and its officers may be fined;
   - directors may be liable to the company for misfeasance and breach of trust;
   - persons receiving funds who knew or ought to have known of the directors' breach of duty will be liable as constructive trustees (*Belmont Finance Corporation v Williams Furniture Ltd (No 2)*).

6.4.11 Reforms

The Company Law Review Steering Group recommend in their *Final Report*:
- the abolition of authorised share capital;
- a new court procedure for capital reduction, to include a requirement for a solvency statement by the directors, and for public companies only, a right to challenge the reduction;
- removal of the prohibition on private companies to give financial assistance for the purchase of their shares;
- revision of some of the exemptions from the prohibition of giving financial assistance and introduction of new exemptions to clarify the law.

6.5 CLASS RIGHTS

6.5.1 General details

1. Different classes of shares will have different rights attached to them, which may be set out in the memorandum or the articles of association. A company may alter its memorandum only as provided by the Act (s2(7)). Section 9 provides that, subject to the provisions of the Act and to conditions contained in the articles, a company may, by special resolution, alter its articles of association. A company cannot deprive itself of its statutory power to alter the articles (*Allen v Gold Reefs of West Africa Ltd* (1900)), *but*
   - if any alteration involves the variation of class rights, then s125 and 127 (designed to give protection to minorities in relation to their class rights) will apply and such rights can only be varied if the proper procedures are followed;
   - if class rights are entrenched in the memorandum of association, variation is more difficult and requires the written consent of all the members of the class or a scheme of arrangement under s425 (see chapter 12).
2. Companies may issues shares such as ordinary shares or preference shares, with different rights attached to them. Class rights will only arise if the company has more than one class of shares. The nature of class rights was considered in *Cumbrian Newspapers Group Ltd v Cumberland and Westmorland Herald Newspaper and Printing Co Ltd* (1986). It was held that rights and benefits may be:
   - rights annexed to particular shares such as the right to a dividend, voting rights;
   - rights conferred on individuals *not* in their capacity as members, i.e. **outsider** rights. These are not class rights.
   - rights conferred on individuals in their capacity as members, but not attached to shares.

   The first and third categories only may be described as class rights.

6.5.2 Variation of class rights

1. The general rule is that rights of one class of shareholders should not be altered by another class.

6.5.3 Class rights in the memorandum

1. If variation is prohibited in the memorandum, then the only way to vary class rights is by a scheme of arrangement under s425.
2. If the memorandum provides a variation procedure, this must be complied with.
3. If the memorandum does not provide for variation, rights may only be varied if *all* members of the company agree to the variation (s125(5)).

6.5.4 Class rights in the articles

This is governed by ss125–7:
1. If articles provide variation of rights procedure, this must be complied with (s125(4)).
2. If the articles do not provide procedure then s125(2) applies. This requires *either*
   - the holders of three quarters of the issued shares of the class in question to consent in writing to the variation; *or*
   - an extraordinary resolution passed at a separate class meeting.
3. Section 127 gives dissenting members of a class who hold at least 15% of shares of that class the right to challenge the variation in court – but they must act within 21 days (and this may cause practical difficulties for shareholders in large companies).

6.5.5 Meaning of 'variation of rights'

The legislation does not make it clear what is meant by 'variation of class rights' but the courts have taken a restrictive view and have sought to distinguish between the rights themselves and the 'enjoyment of the rights'. It may thus be possible to make rights less effective without any technical 'variation' of rights (*White v Bristol Aeroplane Co* (1953); *Greenhalgh v Arderne Cinemas* (1946)).

6.5.6 Reform

The Company Law Steering Group (*Final Report*) recommends:
- the retention of the current provisions on the alteration of class rights, **but**
- that a 75% majority should be required for any alteration of class rights unless a higher majority is stipulated in the company's constitution.

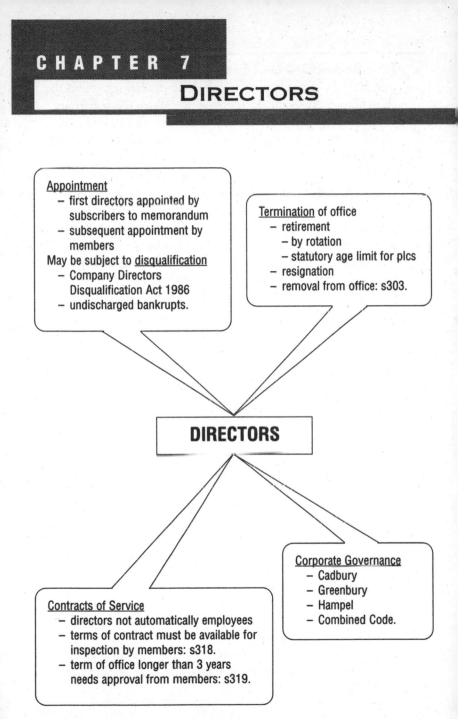

Appointment
- first directors appointed by subscribers to memorandum
- subsequent appointment by members

May be subject to **disqualification**
- Company Directors Disqualification Act 1986
- undischarged bankrupts.

Termination of office
- retirement
  - by rotation
  - statutory age limit for plcs
- resignation
- removal from office: s303.

DIRECTORS

Contracts of Service
- directors not automatically employees
- terms of contract must be available for inspection by members: s318.
- term of office longer than 3 years needs approval from members: s319.

Corporate Governance
- Cadbury
- Greenbury
- Hampel
- Combined Code.

7.1 INTRODUCTION

1. A company is an artificial person and as such can only act through agents.
2. Every private company must have at least one director and a plc must have two.
3. Under s741(1) 'director' means any person carrying out the role of director, by whatever term described, and includes a 'shadow director'.
4. The Act does not require companies to be managed by the directors, but Table A provides for this by article 70 (see below) and most companies will have a similar provision.
5. Every company must keep a register of directors and secretaries at its registered office and must notify the Registrar of Companies of any changes within 14 days.

7.2 APPOINTMENT

Provisions relating to the appointment of directors, maximum and minimum numbers, quoracy, whether the chairman has a casting vote, and similar matters will be included in the company's Articles of Association.

7.2.1 Who appoints directors?

1. The first directors are appointed by a statement in the prescribed form signed by the subscribers of the memorandum. The statement must also be signed by the directors to show that they consent to the appointment.
2. Subsequent directors are appointed by members by ordinary resolution (*Woolf v East Nigel Gold Mining Co Ltd* (1905)).
3. The power to appoint directors may be limited by the Articles. Table A gives power to appoint to both members (art.78) and directors (art.79) but provides that directors appointed by the board can hold office only until the next AGM.

7.2.2 Defective appointment and disqualification

1. S285 provides that the acts of a director are valid even if there is a defect in his or her appointment or qualification. However, s285 does not apply when there has been no appointment at all (*Morris v Kanssen* (1946)).
2. Certain persons may be disqualified from acting as directors:
   - anyone who is the subject of a disqualification order under the Company Directors Disqualification Act 1986;
   - it is an offence of strict liability, triable either way, for an undischarged bankrupt to act as a director without the leave of the court (*R v Brockley* (1994));
   - a sole director cannot also be the company secretary.

7.3 TERMINATION OF OFFICE

7.3.1 Retirement and resignation

1. Under Table A:
   - all directors must retire at the first AGM (art.73), but may seek reappointment (art.80);
   - one third of directors must retire by rotation each year (art.73), but may seek reappointment (art.80).
2. S293 provides that a director of a public company is deemed to retire at the end of the AGM after he or she turns 70, unless the articles provide otherwise.
3. A director may resign by giving notice to the company which the company must accept. Table A requires such notice to be in writing.

7.3.2 Removal from office

1. Directors (either individually or as a board) may be removed by the shareholders by ordinary resolution (s303).
2. Conditions for removal are that:
   - special notice must be given of resolution to remove director;

- a copy must be supplied to the director who is the subject of the resolution;
- the director is entitled to make representations and be heard at the meeting;
- the section shall not deprive the director of any claim for compensation or damages payable in respect of his removal.

3. Shareholders' right to remove directors as set out in s303 apply notwithstanding any provision to the contrary in the company's constitution, but see *Bushell v Faith* (1969).
4. Removal of a director under s303 may incur liability for breach of any contract of service which may exist between the company and the director (*Southern Foundries v Shirlaw* (1940); *Shindler v Northern Raincoat Co Ltd* (1960); *Read v Astoria Garage (Sreatham) Ltd* (1952)).

7.4 REMUNERATION

1. Directors are not entitled to remuneration unless provided for in the constitution (*Hutton v West Cork Railway Co* (1883)).
2. Provision is usually made in the articles – Table A art.82.

7.4.1 Directors as employees

1. Directors are not automatically employees of their companies. A director (especially an executive director) may have a separate contract of service with the company.
2. Whether a director is an employee or not is a question of fact (*Secretary of State for Trade and Industry v Bottrill* (1999)).
3. Terms of a director's contract of service must be available for inspection by members (s318).
4. A term in a director's contract which provides that the director shall be employed for more than five years which cannot be terminated by notice by the company must be approved by the general meeting (s319).
5. *Proposed reform:* The Law Commission recommends that the term of office in s319 should be reduced from five to three years.

7.5 DIVISION OF POWER BETWEEN THE GENERAL MEETING AND THE BOARD

7.5.1 Table A, Article 70

1. Table A provides that, subject to the Act and to any provisions in the company's memorandum and articles of association, the business of the company shall be managed by the directors 'who may exercise all the powers of the company'. The article also provides that the shareholders may give directions to the directors by special resolution.

2. Where the general management of the company is vested in the directors (as in art. 70), the shareholders have no power by ordinary resolution to give directions to the Board or overrule their business decisions (*Automatic Self-Cleansing Filter Syndicate Co Ltd v Cuninghame* (1906); *John Shaw & Sons (Salford) Ltd v Shaw* (1935)).

3. The right to litigate on behalf of the company is an aspect of management and as such is also vested in the board of directors (*Breckland Group Holdings v London & Suffolk Properties Ltd* (1989)).

7.5.2 Default powers of the general meeting

1. The general meeting may ratify an act of the directors which is voidable as an irregular exercise of their powers (*Bamford v Bamford* (1970).

2. The company in general meeting may act if there is no board competent or able to exercise the powers conferred on it (*Baron v Potter* (1914)).

7.5.3 Powers granted to shareholders

Some functions and powers are specifically reserved to the general meeting by the Companies Act or the articles. Included are:

- the power to ratify breaches of duty by directors who act outside their powers (*Bamford v Bamford* (1969));
- the power to alter the articles under s9 by special resolution;
- the power to alter the objects clause under s4;
- the power to appoint directors;
- the power to remove directors under s303.

7.6 CORPORATE GOVERNANCE

1. It can be seen from the above that directors have great powers.
2. The provisions of the Companies Act reserve certain powers to shareholders, but these are often theoretical rather than real.
3. It is unrealistic to believe that in large public companies individual shareholders have any real influence on the management of the company.
4. High profile examples of corporate mismanagement (BCCI, Maxwell) reinforced the need for a framework of regulation which sets out principles of corporate governance.
5. This has been recommended by various reports:
   - In 1992 the Cadbury Committee published its *Report on the Financial Aspects of Corporate Governance.*
   - This was followed in 1995 by the Greenbury *Report on Directors' Remuneration.*
   - In 1998 the Hampel Committee published its *Final Report* and, in consultation with the Stock Exchange produced the *Combined Code* which contains principles of good governance and a code of good practice. Companies listed on the London Stock Exchange are required to include in their annual reports a statement of how they have applied these principles and must give reasons for any failure to comply with the Code.

7.6.1 Some principles of corporate governance relating to directors

The Combined Code contains a number of principles of corporate governance:
1. Every listed company should be headed by an effective board which should lead and control the company.
2. There should be a clear division of responsibilities between the Chairman and the Chief Executive.
3. The board should include a balance of executive and non-executive directors, so that no individual or group of individuals can dominate the board's decision-making.
4. There should be a formal and transparent procedure for the appointment of new directors to the board.
5. All directors should be required to submit themselves for re-election at least every three years.
6. Levels of remuneration should be sufficient to attract and retain the directors needed to run the company successfully, but companies should avoid paying more than necessary.
7. Companies should have a formal and transparent procedure for developing policy on executive remuneration.
8. The company's annual report should contain a statement of remuneration policy and details of the remuneration of each director.

7.6.2 Power and accountability

Directors have great powers. This chapter has dealt with some of these powers and some of the company law and other ways of making directors accountable for their actions. The following chapters continue this theme and you may find it useful to return to the diagram when you have completed your revision.

Duties & Accountability

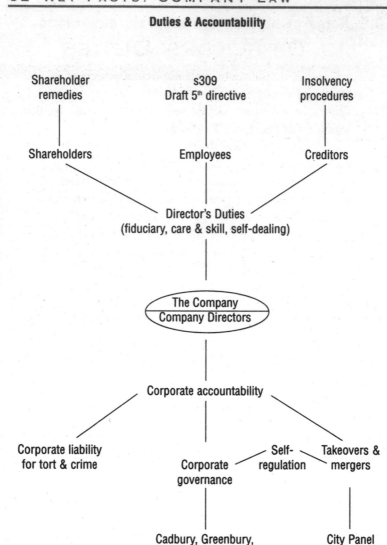

CHAPTER 8

DIRECTORS' DUTIES

8.1 INTRODUCTION

Type of duty	Source	In outline...	Special points – aide memoire
Duties of care and skill	Common law – negligence	Standard of care: traditionally undemanding; subjective test Re *City Equitable Fire Insurance Co Ltd*	Note development of law: influence of s214 Insolvency Act 1986 Re *Theodore Goddard* Re *d'Jan of London* *Dorchester Finance v Stebbing*
Fiduciary duties	Equity – based on fiduciary relationship between directors and company	* Duty to act bona fide in best interest of company * duty to exercise powers for a proper purpose *Hogg v Cramphorn, Howard Smith v Ampol* * duty not to fetter discretion *Fulham Football Club v Cabra*	Liability may not be excluded
No conflict/ no profit rules	Equity	* Personal interests must not conflict with those of company * May not make secret profit: *Cook v Deeks* *Regal (Hastings) v Gulliver* * use of corporate opportunity *IDC v Cooley*	Rules may be relaxed by provision in Articles – Art.85 Table A s317 Companies Act 1985 provides for disclosure to board of directors when company a party to transaction Note relationship of Art85 and s317
Provisions against self-dealing	Statute – Part X Companies Act 1985	Disclosure – s317 substantial property transactions – s320 contracts for loans and guarantees – s330	Note: * exceptions to ss320 and 330 * civil penalties *criminal sanctions * overlap with no conflict/no profit rule

Duties are imposed on directors by the general law and by statute. Directors owe fiduciary duties and duties of care and skill, while Part X of the Companies Act 1985 contains a complex framework of rules relating to self-dealing, disclosure and ratification. The Law Commission, in Consultation Paper No 153 *Company Directors: Regulating Conflicts of Interests and Formulating a Statement of Duties*, undertook a major review of the law, which it found to be over-complex and inaccessible. Wide-ranging reforms were suggested.

8.2 DUTIES OF CARE AND SKILL

1. Directors owe a duty of competence to the company, but historically the standard of care expected of them has been undemanding (*Re Brazilian Rubber Plantations and Estates Ltd* (1911)). Reasons for this approach included:
   - directors were sometimes appointed more because of their social standing than because they had particular skills or qualifications;
   - the courts did not wish to deter people from becoming company directors by imposing onerous duties of care and skill.
2. This duty was categorised into three propositions by Romer J in *Re City Equitable Fire Insurance Co* (1925):
   a) A director is expected to show a degree of care and skill as may reasonably be expected from a person of his/her knowledge and experience. *Note* that the standard of care test is expressed in *subjective* terms, so a director is only expected to act with the degree of care and skill which he or she happens to possess and is not expected to have any particular qualifications or any experience of the company's area of business.
   b) A director is not bound to give continuous attention to the affairs of the company (*Re Cardiff Savings Bank* (1892)).
   c) Subject to normal business practice, directors may leave routine conduct of business affairs in the hands of management.

3. In more recent cases a more robust approach is discernable (*Dorchester Finance v Stebbing* (1989); *Norman v Theodore Goddard* (1991); *Re d'Jan of London Ltd* (1994) and the Australian case *AWA v Daniels* (1992)).

4. The test which has been applied in some cases has an objective element, based on S214(4) Insolvency Act 1986:
   - the general knowledge, skill and experience that may reasonably be expected of a person carrying out the same functions as are carried out by that director in relation to the company, and
   - the general knowledge, skill and experience that that director has.

5. Development of the law has been influenced by, for example:
   - expectation of a more professional approach to company directorship than existed in the first half of the twentieth century;
   - appointment of appropriately qualified people to designated executive directorships – e.g. finance director;
   - contracts of service for executive directors which contain clauses relating to care and skill.

8.3 FIDUCIARY DUTIES

1. It is well established that directors are fiduciaries, owing duties to the company, not to individual shareholders (*Percival v Wright* (1902)). This causes problems of enforcement (see Chapter 10) and the rule in *Foss v Harbottle*.

2. In the New Zealand case *Coleman v Myers* (1977) it was established that in certain circumstances directors may owe a duty to individual shareholders.

3. In *Howard Smith Ltd v Ampol Petroleum* (1974) the general principle was established that if directors issue information to shareholders, for example in a takeover situation, they have a duty to ensure that such information is complete and accurate.

4. In general, directors do not owe duties to the company's creditors, but if a company is insolvent, it has been held that they must have regard to the interest of creditors (*West Mercia Safetywear Ltd v Dodd* (1988)).

5. Different writers classify fiduciary duties in various ways. Some take the view that there is one fundamental duty – the duty to act in good faith for the benefit of the company and that conduct which falls into any of the categories set out below will be a breach of that duty. Others identify separate duties which have emerged in the application of the general principle that directors owe fiduciary duties to the company.

8.3.1 Good faith

1. Directors must act in good faith in what they believe to be the best interests of the company.

2. The duty is subjective: what the directors themselves consider is in the interest of the company (*Re Smith & Fawcett Ltd* (1942)).

3. This is another example of the reluctance of judges to become involved in consideration of commercial decisions taken by company directors. ' The best interests of the company' does not only mean the company as a separate entity, but includes the interests of shareholders as a body.

4. In addition, s309 CA 1985 provides that directors must have regard to 'the interests of the Company's employees in general as well as the interests of members'.

8.3.2 Exercise of powers

1. They must not exercise the powers conferred on them for purposes different from those for which they were conferred.

2. Transactions entered into by the company's directors must be *intra vires*. This is now covered by s35 CA 1985 (see chapter 4).

3. If powers are given to directors for a particular purpose they must not be used for some other purpose and directors must

not use their powers to further their own personal interests (*Lee Panavision Ltd v Lee Lighting Ltd* (1992)).

4. A number of cases involve the allotment of shares. It is a breach of duty to allot shares to avoid a takeover (*Hogg v Cramphorn Ltd* (1967)) or to alter the weight of shareholder votes to influence the outcome of a takeover bid (*Howard Smith Ltd v Ampol Ltd* (1974)).

5. But note that acts in breach of the proper purpose rule can be ratified (*Bamford v Bamford* (1970)).

8.3.3 No fetter on discretion

1. They must not fetter their discretion as to how they shall act, but note that it is not a breach of duty for directors to enter into a binding contract which may have the effect of fettering their discretion at a later date, if they believe the agreement to be in the best interests of the company (*Fulham Football Club v Cabra Estates plc* (1994)) (*Dawsons International plc v Coats Patons plc* (1989)).

8.4 CONFLICTS OF INTEREST AND SECRET PROFITS

Company directors have enormous powers within their companies, and wide opportunity to abuse their position. Self-dealing is regulated by the no-conflict and no-profit rules as well as under Part X of the Companies Act 1985.

8.4.1 The no-conflict rule

1. The general principle was stated in *Aberdeen Railway Company v Blaikie Bros* (1854):

'...it is a rule of universal application that no one, having such (fiduciary) duties to discharge, shall be allowed to enter into engagements in which he has, or can have, a personal interest conflicting, or which possibly may conflict, with the interests of those whom he is bound to protect.'

2. A director must not compete with his or her company (*Hivac v Park Royal* (1946)).

3. The consequences of conflict of interest are:
   - the contract is voidable;
   - the director must account for any gains.

4. But note that a director may enter into a transaction in which he has a conflict of interest if s/he has the informed consent of shareholders in general meeting.

5. Statutory disclosure – s317 CA 1985 imposes a duty to disclose any interest in a contract or a proposed contract with the company to the board of directors. Failure to disclose under s317 does not affect the validity of the contract, but the director concerned may be fined.

6. This applies even in the case of a company with a sole director (*Neptune (Vehicle Washing Equipment) Ltd v Fitzgerald* (1995)).

7. Disclosure must be to an independent board and the function of receiving disclosures cannot be delegated to a committee of the board (*Guinness plc v Saunders* (1990)).

8. A company's Articles of Association may allow directors to enter into such transactions where the interest is disclosed – see Article 85 Table A.

9. If the company's articles include a requirement to disclose, failure to do so will be a breach of duty under the articles and will make the contract voidable.

8.4.2 The no-profit rule

1. A person who is in a fiduciary position must not, without disclosure, make a profit from that position (*Cook v Deeks* (1916); *Regal (Hastings) v Gulliver* (1942)).

2. The rule is strict and it is sufficient that the director makes a profit: there is no need for the company to make a corresponding loss.

3. The use of a corporate opportunity is a particular example of profit-making by directors. A corporate opportunity is regarded as a corporate asset, which directors may not use for their own benefit.
4. This applies even if it would be impossible for the company itself to make use of the opportunity (*Industrial Development Consultants Ltd v Cooley* (1972).
5. However, this rule has been relaxed, for example in *Island Export Finance Ltd v Umunna* (1986).

8.4.3 Relief from liability

1. Any attempt to exempt a director from liability for breach of duty by a provision in the articles or other document is void (s310 CA1985).
2. By virtue of s310(3) a company can insure its directors against liability for breach of duty, but not for any criminal liability.
3. In an action involving breach of duty, a court may relieve a director of liability, in whole or in part, if the director has acted honestly and it appears to the court that s/he should be excused in the light of all the circumstances (s727 CA 1985), see for example *Re Duomatic Ltd* (1969).

8.5 SELF-DEALING – STATUTORY PROVISIONS

There are a number of statutory provisions in Part X which reinforce and sometimes appear to overlap with directors' fiduciary duties.

Section	Summary	Penalty
s317	Directors must disclose any interest in a contract with the company at a meeting of the board of directors	Fine (s317(7))
s318	Directors' service contracts are open to inspection	Fine (s318(8))
s319	Director's contract for more than 5 years must be approved by resolution of general meeting	Any term contravening s319 is void
s320	Substantial property transactions: directors shall not acquire substantial non-cash assets from the company and the company shall not acquire such assets from directors unless approved by the general meeting (note exceptions – s321)	Transaction is voidable at option of company – Directors liable to account or to indemnify company s322(3)

8.5.1 Loans to Directors: ss330–341

1. A company may not make a loan in total to one of its directors or a director of its holding company.
2. A company may not give a guarantee or provide collateral security for a loan made by someone else to one of its directors or to a director of its holding company.
3. Any transaction which contravenes s330 (to which there are exceptions) is voidable by the company unless a third party has acquired rights bona fide for value without notice.

8.6 PROPOSALS FOR REFORM

1. The law on directors' duties is a complex web of common law, fiduciary and statutory rules and principles, some of

which overlap and which are sometimes not entirely consistent with one another.

2. The reform of the law has been the subject of extensive review and consultation by the Law Commission and the Company Law Review Steering Group.

3. The following issues, associated with the reform of company law as a whole, were considered by the Law Commission in their Consultation Paper no. 153 *Regulating Conflicts of Interest:*
   - efficiency
   - overregulation
   - self-regulation
   - legislation drafting
   - codification
   - decriminalisation
   - EC harmonisation.

4. A number of proposals for reform were made and the Commission sought views on the following options:
   - comprehensive codification of the law of directors' duties;
   - partial codification of the law;
   - a statutory statement of guidance, which would not replace the general law;
   - a non-binding statement of the major duties to be inserted into various official documents, e.g. annual accounts;
   - authoritative pamphlets summarising the duties of directors.

5. Following consultation, in *Company Directors: Regulating Conflicts of Interest and Formulating a Statement of Duties* (Law Com No 261 1999) the Law Commission recommended:
   - codification of the main duties of company directors;
   - that the statutory provisions should be printed on the form signed by directors on appointment.

8.6.1 Company Law Steering Group Final Report

1. The *Final Report* adopts the proposal for codification and contains a proposed clause and a Schedule. The clause

provides that a company director owes a duty to the company to comply with the Schedule.

2. The proposed Schedule contains several general principles applying to a director in relation to the performance of his or her functions as a director and transactions with third parties:
   - obeying the constitution;
   - promotion of the company's objectives;
   - exercising independent judgment and not delegating powers;
   - exercise of care, skill and diligence;
   - not entering transactions involving a conflict of interest;
   - not making personal use of company's property, information or opportunity;
   - not accepting benefits from third parties;
   - special duties to protect creditors when the company is likely not to be able to pay its debts.

3. In relation to negligence, the standard of care should include both objective and subjective elements.

4. The Steering Group also adopts the proposal that a statement of duties should be signed by directors on appointment, and has produced a draft statement of principles governing directors in the performance of their duties.

CHAPTER 9
INSIDER DEALING

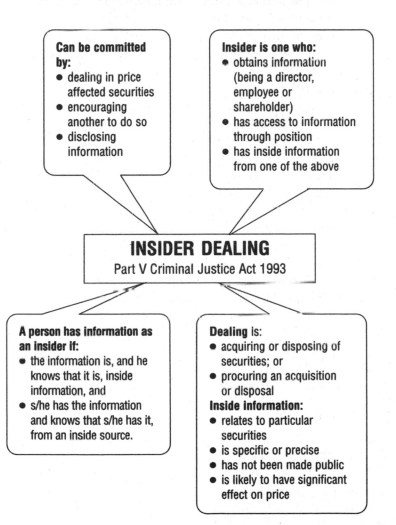

Can be committed by:
- dealing in price affected securities
- encouraging another to do so
- disclosing information

Insider is one who:
- obtains information (being a director, employee or shareholder)
- has access to information through position
- has inside information from one of the above

INSIDER DEALING
Part V Criminal Justice Act 1993

A person has information as an insider if:
- the information is, and he knows that it is, inside information, and
- s/he has the information and knows that s/he has it, from an inside source.

Dealing is:
- acquiring or disposing of securities; or
- procuring an acquisition or disposal

Inside information:
- relates to particular securities
- is specific or precise
- has not been made public
- is likely to have significant effect on price

9.1 INTRODUCTION

1. Insider dealing has been defined by Farrar as 'The use by an insider of price-sensitive information (known to him but not generally and which he has acquired by virtue of his position) to trade to his advantage in the securities of a company.'

2. In recent years such conduct has been seen as a breach of trust by a person in a fiduciary position and as a fraud on other investors. Accordingly, since 1980, it has been a criminal offence. The law was revised in the Company Securities (Insider Dealing) Act 1985 and amended by the Financial Services Act 1986.

3. In 1989, an EC directive (89/592/EEC) was adopted, which required that certain changes be made to the UK law. The new law, now more focused on control of securities markets than on abuse of confidential information, is contained in the Criminal Justice Act 1993.

4. Some commentators argue against the criminalisation of insider dealing. Professor H.G. Manne in particular has put up a defence of the practice on the grounds that:
   - insider dealing should be seen as a legitimate benefit of management and a reward for entrepreneurial ability;
   - it is a 'victimless crime' since the transaction would have taken place whether or not one party had inside information;
   - it brings information to the market quickly;
   - it is notoriously difficult to prove and enforce and it is therefore futile to have the offence on the statute book.

   However, these arguments have not been widely accepted.

9.2 THE OFFENCE

1. The offence itself is set out in s52 CJA 1993, and the terms used in s52 are defined in sections 54–60. Under s52 an individual, who has information as an insider, may commit the offence in three ways:

- s52(1) dealing in price affected securities as principal or agent;
- s52(2) (a) encouraging another to do so;
- s52(2) (b) disclosing information otherwise than in the proper performance of his functions.

2. The offence extends only to regulated markets, or in circumstances where the person dealing relies on a professional intermediary or is himself a professional intermediary.

9.2.1 Dealing

1. Section 55(1) provides that a person deals if he:
   - acquires or disposes of the securities (whether as principal or agent) *or*
   - procures, directly or indirectly, an acquisition or disposal of the securities by any other person.

9.2.2 Inside information

Under s56, inside information:
- relates to particular securities or to a particular issue of securities... not to securities generally;
- is specific or precise;
- has not been made public;
- would be likely to have a significant effect on the price of any securities if it were made public.

9.2.3 Price affected securities

... are securities whose price is likely to be significantly affected if an item of inside information were made public.

9.2.4 Who can commit the offence?

1. Under s57 the offence can be committed only by a person who has information as an insider, i.e.:

- has information (which is, and which s/he knows is, inside information) as an insider, *or*
- has the information, and knows that he has it from an inside source.

2. An **insider** is defined as
   - an individual who obtains information through being a director, employee or shareholder of the issuer of securities, *or*
   - an individual who has access to information by virtue of his employment, office or profession, whether or not employment is with the issuer of securities, or
   - those who have inside information 'the direct or indirect source of which is a person falling into either of the first two categories'.

3. The wording of this section is different from that in Company Securities (Insider Dealing) Act 1985, which required, in the case of a tippee, that the information had been 'knowingly obtained'. The difficulties discussed in *Attorney General's Reference No 1 of 1988* (1989) have been overcome by the rewording.

4. There is an exemption for market makers in relation to dealing or encouraging other provided s to deal by s53(4), as long as they act in good faith and in the normal course of business.

9.2.5 When is information made public?

1. Under s58(1) information is made public if:
   - it is published in accordance with the rules of a regulated market for the purpose of informing investors and their professional advisers;
   - it is contained in records which are open to inspection by the public;
   - it can be readily acquired by those likely to deal in any securities to which the information relates, or of an issuer to which the information relates;
   - it is derived from information which has been made public.

2. S58(3) is also relevant and provides that information may be treated as made public even though

- it can only be acquired by persons exercising diligence or expertise;
- it is communicated to a section of the public and not to the public at large;
- it can be acquired only by observation;
- it is communicated only on payment of a fee;
- it is published only outside the United Kingdom.

9.2.6 Defences

1. Section 53 provides the following defences in relation to both dealing and encouraging:

- that s/he did not expect the dealing to result in a profit (or avoid a loss) attributable to the fact that the information was price sensitive;
- that s/he reasonably believed that the information had been disclosed;
- that s/he would have done what he did even if he had not had the information.

2. In relation to disclosing the defences are:

- that s/he did not expect any person to deal in the securities because of the disclosure;
- that s/he did not expect the dealing to result in a profit attributable to the fact that the information was price sensitive.

9.2.7 Penalties and procedure

1. The offence is triable either way.

2. Maximum penalty on conviction on indictment is seven years imprisonment and/or a fine on which there is no limits. 61(1). *R v Collier* (1987, unreported)) is one of the few convictions leading to imprisonment.

3. Any transaction entered into in contravention of the act will stand.

9.2.8 Procedure

A prosecution can be instituted only by or with the consent of the Secretary of State for Trade and Industry or the DPP.

9.3 UK LISTING AUTHORITY MODEL CODE

1. Listed companies in the UK must have internal rules to govern dealings in securities by its directors, which must be at least as rigorous as the UKLA Model Code.
2. The Code lays down a number of principles to be followed by directors when dealing in their companies' securities, including the following:
   - A director of a listed company must notify the chairman (or another designated director) in advance of dealing in the company's securities. Dealings by the chairman or designated director must be notified to the board. A record of notifications and clearances must be kept.
   - A director of a listed company must not buy the company's securities during a 'close period', that is the two months before the preliminary announcements of its half-yearly and annual results or the month before the announcement of its quarterly results.

9.4 CIVIL LIABILITY

1. It has been argued that insider dealing should give rise to civil liability as well as criminal prosecution. Difficulties arise because it is often not possible to establish who suffered the loss or to quantify the loss.
2. The Financial Services and Markets Act 2000, when fully implemented will provide for civil liability in cases involving market abuse.

CHAPTER 10
SHAREHOLDER REMEDIES

10.1 THE RULE IN *FOSS V HARBOTTLE*

1. Responsibility for decision-making in a company lies with either the board of directors or the shareholders in general meeting, by consent of the majority.
2. A company is recognised as a separate legal person, so if a wrong is done to the company, the proper person to sue the wrongdoer is the company itself: this is the rule in *Foss v Harbottle* (1843).
3. There are said to be two elements to the rule:
   - the proper plaintiff in an action in respect of a wrong alleged to be done to a company is the company itself;
   - where the alleged wrong is a transaction which could be made binding on the company by a simple majority of the members, no individual member can bring an action in respect of that transaction (*Edwards v Halliwell* (1950)).
4. This can lead to difficulty if the wrongdoers are in control of the company, since it would normally be those in control who would instigate legal action on behalf of the company (Table A, art.70, *Breckland Group Holdings Ltd v London & Suffolk Property Holdings Ltd* (1989)).
5. For that reason the courts may exceptionally allow an individual shareholder to bring an action on behalf of the company.

10.2 SHAREHOLDER REMEDIES: THE COMMON LAW

Common law remedies

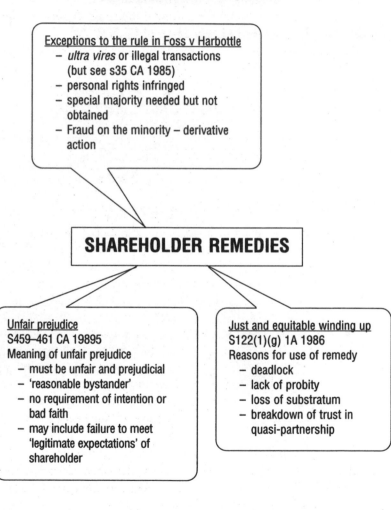

Exceptions to the rule in Foss v Harbottle
- *ultra vires* or illegal transactions (but see s35 CA 1985)
- personal rights infringed
- special majority needed but not obtained
- Fraud on the minority – derivative action

SHAREHOLDER REMEDIES

Unfair prejudice
S459–461 CA 19895
Meaning of unfair prejudice
- must be unfair and prejudicial
- 'reasonable bystander'
- no requirement of intention or bad faith
- may include failure to meet 'legitimate expectations' of shareholder

Just and equitable winding up
S122(1)(g) 1A 1986
Reasons for use of remedy
- deadlock
- lack of probity
- loss of substratum
- breakdown of trust in quasi-partnership

Statutory remedies

10.2.1 Personal and derivative claims

1. An individual shareholder may instigate litigation to enforce **personal** rights.
2. Membership rights may arise in a number of ways but it is important to consider the nature of the contract between the company and its members under s14 CA 1985.
3. A **derivative** claim is one where the right of action is derived from the company and is exercised on behalf of the company.
4. A derivative claim arises only when proceedings cannot be taken in the name of the company itself, because:
   * the directors have decided not to sue;
   * the members have decided not to sue, in circumstances where they have the power to initiate litigation;
   * the shareholders have ratified the act in question.

10.2.2 Restrictions on derivative claims

1. The courts have been reluctant to allow the widespread use of derivative claims for the following reasons:
   * the concept of majority rule;
   * judicial reluctance to become involved in disputes over management and business policy;
   * floodgates argument;
   * difficulties of proof, leading to protracted litigation;
   * cost – who pays? The company will benefit if the action succeeds, but does not want to undertake litigation (*Wallersteiner v Moir (No 2)* (1975)). In appropriate circumstances the courts will make a Wallersteiner order, ordering the company to pay;
   * trial of preliminary issue – extends the proceedings.
2. A restrictive view of the scope of the derivative claim has been taken (*Prudential Assurance Ltd v Newman Industries* (1981); *Smith v Croft* (1986)).

3. A derivative claim will not be allowed to proceed if:
- a more appropriate way of dealing with the matter is available (*Cooke v Cooke* (1997)), where the claimant had also petitioned under s459 CA 1985 (see below);
- the claimant is making the claim for personal reasons rather than for the benefit of the company (*Barrett v Duckett* (1995)).

10.2.3 Exceptions to the rule in *Foss v Harbottle*

1. Where the transaction is *ultra vires* or illegal – this exception has been circumscribed by s35 CA 1985.
2. Where the transaction requires a special majority (*Edwards v Halliwell*).
3. Where personal rights of a shareholder are infringed, for example:
   a) dividends paid in the form of bonds when the articles required payment in cash: (*Wood v Odessa Waterworks Co* (1889));
   b) a member's vote improperly rejected by the chairman of a general meeting (*Pender v Lushington* (1877));
   c) failure by directors to allow a veto of a decision as provided in the articles (*Quin & Axtens Ltd v Salmon* (1909)).
4. In all the above cases, a member has a personal right to take legal proceedings.
5. The one exception to the rule where the member takes legal proceedings deriving from the company and on behalf of the company is where the transaction amounts to a fraud on the minority; the shareholder must establish 'fraud'.
6. The shareholder must show that the wrongdoers are in control of the company.

10.2.4 What is fraud in this context?

1. This includes fraud in the wide sense of a misuse of power, for example:
- directors using company property to benefit themselves

(*Alexander v Automatic Telephone Co* (1900));
- directors diverting company business for their own advantage (*Cook v Deeks* (1916));
- using voting power not for the benefit of the company but for the benefit of the majority and to the disadvantage of the minority (*Estmanco (Kilner House) Ltd v Greater London Council* (1982)).

2. Negligence on its own does not amount to fraud (*Pavlides v Jensen* (1956)).

3. But 'self-seeking' negligence where the defendant has benefited from the transaction is within the meaning of fraud (*Daniels v Daniels* (1978)).

10.2.5 Wrongdoer control

It must be established that the company is not able to institute proceedings in its own name.

10.2.6 Proposed Reforms

1. The Law Commission recommended (*Shareholder Remedies*) that certain matters should be taken into account by the court when considering an application to continue a derivative claim:
- whether the claimant is acting in good faith;
- whether the claim is in the interests of the company;
- whether the activity in question may be approved by the company in general meeting and whether it has been so approved;
- whether the company in general meeting has resolved not to pursue the cause of action;
- the opinion of an independent organ that, for commercial reasons, the claim should or should not be pursued;
- whether an alternative remedy is available.

2. The Company Law Steering Group *Final Report* recommends that these matters should be left to the discretion of the court.

3. More generally, the Law Commission recorded a number of criticisms of the rule in *Foss v Harbottle* and the derivative claim. It recommended partial abolition of the rule and a new derivative claim. This view was accepted by the Company Law Steering Group. The *Final Report* recommends that derivative claims should be restricted to breaches of directors' duties and that they should be put on a statutory footing.

10.3 STATUTORY PROVISIONS: UNFAIR PREJUDICE

S459(1) CA 1985 provides that a member may petition the court 'on the ground that the company's affairs are being or have been conducted in a manner which is unfairly prejudicial to the interests of its members...' This section (first enacted as s75 CA 1980) replaced the very restrictive remedy under s210 CA 1948 which provided a remedy for 'oppressive' conduct.

10.3.1 Who can petition?

1. A claim may be made by:
- members of the company;
- those to whom shares have been transferred by operation of law, for example personal representatives, trustees in bankruptcy.

2. There is no requirement of 'clean hands' (in contrast to the remedy under s122(1)(g) Insolvency Act 1986) although the conduct of the petitioner may affect the remedy (*Re London School of Electronics* (1986)).

10.3.2 Meaning of 'unfairly prejudicial conduct'

1. Conduct must be both unfair and prejudicial (*Re BSB Holdings Ltd (No 2)* (1996)).

2. However, in contrast to the way the courts interpreted s210 of the 1948 Act, the terms 'unfair' and 'prejudicial' have been given a very wide interpretation.

3. The courts have employed the concept of the reasonable bystander in determining unfair prejudice.

4. There is no need, in proving unfairness, to show either intention or bad faith (*Re RA Noble & Sons (Clothing) Ltd* (1983)).

5. Prejudice does not necessarily require a reduction in the value of the petitioner's shareholding and may be shown in a number of ways:

    a) exclusion from management (*Richards v Lundy* (2000));

    b) failure to pay dividends P (*Re Sam Weller & Sons Ltd* (1990));

    c) excessive remuneration to directors;

    d) diversion of corporate assets or corporate opportunity (*Re London School of Electronics Ltd* (1986));

    e) Packing the board with directors having interests adverse to the company (*Whyte, Petitioner* (1984)).

6. In general, mismanagement will not amount to unfair prejudice (*Re Elgindata Ltd* (1991)), but serious or gross mismanagement has been considered prejudicial (*Re Macro (Ipswich) Ltd* (1994)).

7. The section has been interpreted to include not only a breach of the company's constitution, but also a failure to meet the 'legitimate expectations' of a member or members. In the case of small private companies, the legitimate expectations may be outside of the constitution (*Re Saul D Harrison & Sons Ltd* (1994); *Richards v Lundy* (2000)). However, the courts have not been willing to recognise legitimate expectations beyond the constitution in the case of public companies (*Re Blue Arrow plc* (1987)).

8. The law in this area has been discussed and clarified by the House of Lords in *O'Neill v Phillips* (1999). The concept of 'legitimate expectation' was applied restrictively on the basis that there was no conclusive agreement between the parties on which it could be based.

10.3.3 The orders of the court

1. It is important to note the scope and flexibility of the orders. The court has freedom to make whatever order is deemed appropriate in the circumstances, but some specific orders are set out in s461. These are:
   - to regulate the company's affairs in future (*Re Harmer Ltd* (1958) – a case heard under the old s210);
   - to order the company to do or refrain from doing something
   - to authorise civil proceedings;
   - to order the purchase of the petitioner's shares.
2. The most common remedy is an order of the court to purchase the shares of the petitioner. The following principles are applied:
   - the shares are normally purchased at a their full value;
   - the conduct of the petitioner (for example if s/he was in any way to blame for the breakdown) may be relevant and the shares may be discounted to reflect this;
   - usually the valuation will be calculated as at the time of the order, but the court has discretion in fixing the date and may fix it at the time of the petition;
   - if the parties cannot agree, the price should be set by an independent valuer.

10.3.4 The future of the remedy?

1. Since its introduction, s459 has given minority shareholders an important remedy.
2. However, it has been criticised for the cost involved in bringing a case, for the length and complexity of cases and for the fact that it may allow minority shareholders to enforce their will over that of the majority.
3. The decision of the House of Lords in *O'Neill v Phillips* is likely to restrict the use of the section.

10.3.5 Proposed reforms

1. In 1996 the Law Commission published a consultation paper (no 142) followed in 1997 by a Report (*Shareholder Remedies* (1997 CM 3769) Law Com No 246.
2. Their main concern was with the length and complexity of the proceedings.
3. The Law Commission recommended that there should be a rebuttable presumption that where a shareholder has been excluded from participation in the management of the company the conduct will be presumed to be unfairly prejudicial by reason of the exclusion; and
   - if the presumption is not rebutted and the court is satisfied that it ought to order a buy-out of the petitioner's shares, it should do so on a pro-rata basis (i.e. without any discount to reflect the fact that the petitioner's holding is a minority holding);
   - winding up should be added to the remedies specified in s461;
   - an 'exit provision' should be included in Table A.
4. The Company Law Steering Group in its *Final Report* does not accept these proposals. It recommends that 'in the interests of certainty and the containment of the scope of section 459 actions', the decision in *O'Neill v Phillips* should be accepted and the basis for a claim under section 459 should be a departure from an agreement.

10.4 WINDING UP ON THE JUST AND EQUITABLE GROUND

1. The Insolvency Act 1986 provides a rather drastic remedy for a dissatisfied shareholder:
2. S122 (1)(g) provides that company may be wound up if the court is of the opinion that it is just and equitable that the company should be wound up.
3. S124 provides that an application can be made by anyone who is a contributory. A contributory is a person who is liable

to contribute to the assets of a company in the event of its being wound up. A fully paid-up member who is not liable to contribute has to show that s/he has a tangible interest in the winding up.

10.4.1 Restrictions on the remedy

1. It is an equitable procedure, and there is therefore the requirement for 'clean hands'.
2. The court will not order a winding up if there is an alternative remedy available to the petitioners and they have been unreasonable in not accepting it (*Re a Company* (No. 002567 of 1982) (1983)). However, there have been circumstances where the alternative remedy has not been appropriate and the application for winding up has succeeded (*Virdi v Abbey Leisure* (1990)).

10.4.2 Reasons for applications for just and equitable winding up

1. Successful petitions have been made on the following grounds:
   - in the case of a quasi-partnership that the relationship of trust and confidence has broken down (*Re Yenidje Tobacco Co Ltd* (1916)). The breach must be sufficiently serious to justify the winding up;
   - deadlock (*Ng Eng Hiam v Hg Kee Wei* (1964));
   - lack of probity (*Loch v John Blackwood Ltd* (1924)). The fact that directors are negligent and inefficient is not sufficient to show lack of probity (*Five Minute Car Wash Service Ltd* (1966));
   - loss of substratum of company (*Re German Date Coffee Co* (1882)).
2. In *Ebrahimi v Westbourne Galleries* (1973) Lord Wilberforce laid down general guidelines in cases involving quasi-partnerships and a breakdown of trust. There must have been:
   - a breakdown of trust and confidence;

- reasonable expectation of taking part in the management of the company;
- a restriction on the sale of shares so that the petitioner is 'locked into' the company.

10.4.3 Scope of the remedy

1. In some cases where unfair prejudice cannot be shown, the court has ordered a winding up (*Re RA Noble (Clothing) Ltd* (1983)).
2. But a petition was refused in *Re Guidesone* on the ground that the proposition that winding up on the just and equitable ground is wider than s459 is inconsistent with *O'Neill v Phillips*.
3. The Law Commission has recommended that winding up should be added to the remedies available under s461 in order to streamline the procedures.

CHAPTER 11
TAKEOVERS AND MERGERS

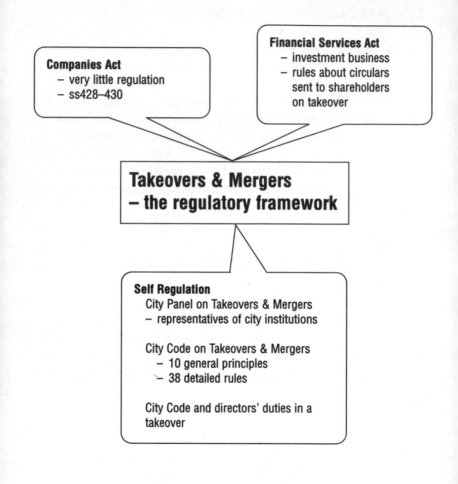

Companies Act
  – very little regulation
  – ss428–430

Financial Services Act
  – investment business
  – rules about circulars
    sent to shareholders
    on takeover

**Takeovers & Mergers
– the regulatory framework**

Self Regulation
  City Panel on Takeovers & Mergers
  – representatives of city institutions

  City Code on Takeovers & Mergers
  – 10 general principles
  – 38 detailed rules

  City Code and directors' duties in a
  takeover

11.1 TAKOVERS

1. A takeover is usually understood to mean the process by which one company gains control of another.
2. 'Control' means the ability to influence policy and control the board of directors, usually requiring more than 50% of the voting shares.
3. **Private companies** often have a provision in the articles of association allowing directors to refuse to register a transfer of shares, so that a takeover will not be possible without the authority and consent of the directors.
4. **Public companies** can offer shares to the public and may be listed on the Stock Exchange. They often have large and dispersed shareholdings. The usual procedure is for the offeror a company to the send circular to the shareholders in offeree (or target) company making an offer to buy their shares. This circular is an 'investment invitation' and is subject to s57 Financial Services Act 1986.

11.2 BUYOUT AND SELLOUT RIGHTS

There are very few company law rules governing takeovers, but the rights of offerors, when the majority of shareholders have accepted a bid, to acquire remaining shareholdings and of minority shareholders to require their shares to be bought out are governed by ss428–430F.

11.2.1 Compulsory acquisition

1. The Companies Act provides a procedure to enable a takeover bidder who has acquired 90% of the shares in a company to acquire the remaining shares compulsorily.
2. 90% means 90% of the shares that are subject to the offer – this excludes shares that are already held by the offeror or associates.
3. **Terms** must be the same as for other shares bid for.
4. **Time limit** – acquisition of 90% must be achieved within four months of the offer being made.

5. If 90% cannot be reached because some shareholders cannot be traced, but would otherwise be reached, then the court may authorise compulsory acquisition if it considers it to be just and equitable.

11.2.2 Intervention by the court

1. A shareholder can apply to the court within six weeks of the offer being made. The court can:
- order that the offeror is not entitled to acquire the shares;
- specify terms different from the offer.

2. Grounds for court intervention: the offer is unfair, despite the fact that 90% have accepted it (*Re Sussex Brick Co Ltd* (1961); *Re Bugle Press Ltd* (1961)).

11.2.3 Requisition by shareholders to buy shares

A procedure is also provided to enable a small minority of shareholders whose shares have not been bought in the takeover to require the offeror to buy them out. Regulations are as follows:
- 90% limit applies as for compulsory acquisition;
- offeror must issue compulsory acquisition notice or notify every shareholder who has not accepted offer of right to be bought out;
- requisition to buyout must be made in writing;
- **terms** must be the same as for all other shares bid for, or agreed by parties, or fixed by the court;
- **time limit** – end of period by which offer can be accepted.

11.3 SELF-REGULATION: THE CITY PANEL

1. The City Panel on Takeovers and Mergers is a self-regulatory body which is responsible for the regulation of takeovers of public companies in the UK within the framework of the self-

regulatory rules contained in the City Code on Takeovers and Mergers.
2. The Panel has no statutory basis or legal powers of enforcement.
3. The panel is composed of:
   - the Chairman and Deputy Chairman, appointed by the Bank of England;
   - members who are representatives of leading City institutions.

11.3.1 Functions of the Panel

1. Legislative – it drafts the provisions of the Code and makes amendments.
2. Interpretive – it interprets the Code.
3. Monitoring/investigative – it establishes whether there has been a breach of the Code.
4. Enforcement – it ensures compliance with the Code.
   - If a breach is suspected, the company concerned is invited to appear before the Panel.
   - If it is shown that a breach has occurred, a private reprimand may be issued, or the company may be reported to another authority, for example the Stock Exchange or the Financial Services Authority.

11.3.2 Judicial Review and the role of the court

1. It has been held that the Panel is subject to judicial review (*R v Panel on Takeovers and Mergers ex parte Datafin* (1987); *R v Panel on Takeovers and Mergers, ex parte Guinness plc* (1990)).
2. The court recognises that the Panel is required to make decisions quickly and may give a ruling for future guidance rather than reverse a past decision.

11.4 THE CITY CODE ON TAKEOVERS AND MERGERS

1. The current edition of the Code was published on 8th July 1993. It is a lengthy document, containing ten General Principles and 38 Rules.
2. The main objective of the Code is:
   - to ensure fair and equal treatment of all shareholders in relation to takeovers;
   - to provide an orderly framework within which takeovers are conducted.
3. The Code is not concerned with:
   - the financial or commercial advantages or disadvantages of a takeover. These are matters for the company and its shareholders;
   - issues such as competition policy, which are the responsibility of government.

11.4.1 Principles underpinning the code

1. There should be equal treatment of all shareholders of a particular class.
2. The same information should be provided to all shareholders.
3. An offeror should only announce an offer after careful and responsible consideration, thus ensuring that offers for takeovers should only be made when the acquiring company believes it can implement the takeover.
4. Shareholders should have full information in order to enable them to consider the merits of a bid and should have it in proper time to enable them to reach a decision.
5. All documentation sent to shareholders containing information or advice must be prepared with the highest standards of care and accuracy, in order to prevent the operation of a false market in shares on the basis of inadequate or inaccurate information.

6. Directors of the target company should obtain approval of members before undertaking any action that could frustrate the offer or prejudice the desirability of the takeover bid.
7. Rights of control must be exercised in good faith and there must be no oppression of a minority.
8. Directors should disregard their own personal interest in the company and consider what would be in the interests of members generally when advising members of the terms of the takeover.
9. Where control of a company is acquired by a person or persons acting in concert, a general offer to all other shareholders is usually required.

11.4.2 Enforcement

The Code does not have the force of law, but works on the premise that 'those who seek to take advantage of the facilities of the securities markets in the United Kingdom should conduct themselves in matters relating to takeovers in accordance with best business standards and so according to the Code' (Introduction to the Code).

11.5 THE CODE AND DIRECTORS' DUTIES

1. Directors owe fiduciary duties to the company (*Hogg v Cramphorn; Howard Smith Ltd v Ampol Petroleum Ltd*).
2. In addition, General Principle 9 of the Code stipulates:
   - directors of an offeror and offeree company must always, in advising their shareholders, act only in their capacity as directors and not have regard to their personal or family shareholdings;
   - directors of the offeree company should give careful consideration before they enter into any commitment with an offeror' which would restrict their freedom to advise their shareholders in the future;

- such commitments may give rise to conflicts of interest or result in a breach of the directors' fiduciary duties.

3. It is established that although directors owe a duty to shareholders to ensure that any information and advice is given in good faith and is not misleading, fiduciary duties are owed to the company (*Dawson International plc v Coats Patons plc* (1988)).

CHAPTER 12

COMPANY FAILURE AND LIQUIDATION

Insolvency & Liquidation

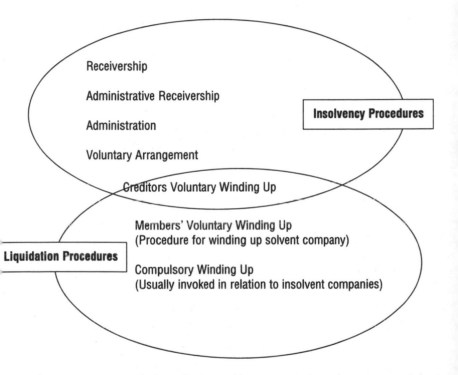

Receivership

Administrative Receivership

Administration

Voluntary Arrangement

Creditors Voluntary Winding Up

Insolvency Procedures

Members' Voluntary Winding Up
(Procedure for winding up solvent company)

Liquidation Procedures

Compulsory Winding Up
(Usually invoked in relation to insolvent companies)

12.1 THE LEGAL FRAMEWORK

1. The law governing insolvency and liquidation was changed
   and updated by the Insolvency Act 1985, following
   recommendations of the Cork Report, and is now contained
   in the Insolvency Act 1986.

2. The changes were intended to introduce procedures to facilitate the survival of a company in financial difficulty.
3. Not all insolvency procedures result in the liquidation of the company and in some circumstances (notably the members' voluntary winding up) a company which is not insolvent will be put into liquidation.
4. The Insolvency Act 2000 will make some modest changes to the law when fully in force.

12.1.1 Objectives of corporate insolvency law

The following objectives have been suggested:
1. To facilitate the recovery of companies in financial difficulty.
2. To suspend the pursuit of rights and remedies of individual creditors.
3. To divest directors of their powers of management.
4. To prevent transfers and transactions which unfairly prejudice the general creditors.
5. To procure an orderly distribution of the estate and a fair system for the ranking of claims.
6. To impose responsibility for culpable management by directors and officers.

12.1.2 Insolvency practitioners

All liquidation and insolvency procedures require the appointment of an insolvency practitioner to a particular office as shown in this chart.

Administrative receivership	Administrative receiver
Administration order	Administrator
Voluntary arrangement	Supervisor
Liquidation (voluntary or compulsory)	Liquidator

12.1.3 Qualification

a) Only an individual can act as an insolvency practitioner, and he or she must not be:
   - an undischarged bankrupt;
   - subject to a director disqualification order;
   - a patient within the meaning of the mental health legislation.

b) He or she must be qualified to act generally:
   recognised professional bodies can authorise persons to act as insolvency practitioners.

c) He or she must be qualified to act in relation to the particular company – s390.

d) A person who acts without being qualified to do so commits a criminal offence.

12.2 INSOLVENCY AND LIQUIDATION PROCEDURES

	Insolvency procedure?	Liquidation procedure?	Court involvement
Company voluntary arrangement (ss1–7 IA1986)	yes	no	Must be reported but does not require approval
Scheme of arrangement under s425 CA 1985	no	no	Court must approve
Administration order (ss8–12) IA 1986	yes	no	Court order required – Administrator appointed by court
Appointment of administrative receiver	yes	no	May be appointed by court, but usually appointed by chargee
Members' voluntary winding up	no	yes	No involvement
Creditors' voluntary winding up	yes	yes	Not usually involved – may give directions on appointment of liquidator
Compulsory winding up	usually	yes	Court makes order following petition

12.2.1 Company voluntary arrangements

1. These are governed by ss1–7 Insolvency Act 1986
2. Company voluntary arrangements: the proposal for a company **not in liquidation**:
   - the directors of a company may propose a composition or scheme of arrangement;
   - they must nominate an insolvency practitioner to act as supervisor;
   - the person nominated must submit a report to the court indicating whether he or she thinks the proposal should be put to meetings of creditors and members;
   - if the nominee thinks the proposal should be put to meetings s/he must call separate meetings of all creditors (whose addresses are known) and members.
3. It is possible that before the arrangement can be agreed, a creditor will petition for a winding up. To prevent this, directors often petition for an administration order, to get a moratorium on payment of the company's debts (see below). When in force the Insolvency Act 2000 will enable the directors of a company to petition for a moratorium at the same time as the proposal for a CVA is made.
4. When a company is **in liquidation** or administration:
   - the liquidator or administrator may propose a composition or scheme of arrangement;
   - he or she may act as supervisor and summon meetings without reference to the court;
   - he or she may nominate another insolvency practitioner, who will submit a report and then call meetings as above.
5. The meetings may approve or modify the proposal, but cannot approve an arrangement which deprives a secured creditor of his right to enforce the security without the consent of the creditor. Nor can they approve a proposal which alters the priority of preferential debts.

6. Once the proposal is approved, it takes effect as if it was made at the creditors meeting, and binds all creditors entitled to vote at that meeting. However, there is a 28-day period within which application may be made to the court to have the proposal set aside.

12.2.2 Scheme of arrangement under s425 Companies Act 1985

1. A compromise or arrangement may also be made under ss425–428 of the Companies Act, under which the rights of both creditors and members can be varied.

2. Under this procedure, a court order is required.

12.2.3 Administration orders

1. A petition may be presented by:
- the company;
- a creditor;
- the supervisor of a voluntary arrangement.

2. The grounds for granting an administration order are:
- The company must be, or be likely to become, unable to pay its debts.
- The company must not be in liquidation or administrative receivership – this provision enables the holder of a floating charge to prevent the making of an administration order by the appointment of an administrative receiver.
- The court must be satisfied that an administration order is likely to achieve one of the following:
  a) the survival of the company and the whole or any part of its undertaking as a going concern;
  b) the approval of a voluntary arrangement under ss1–7 IA 1986;
  c) the approval of a scheme of arrangement under s425 CA 1985;
  d) a more advantageous realisation of the company's assets than would be effected on a winding up.

3. The administrator must formulate a proposal for dealing with the company which must be submitted to unsecured creditors within three months of appointment.

12.2.4 Receivers and administrative receivers: appointment

1. A receiver is an individual appointed to take control of property which is security for a debt.
2. Receivers may be appointed by the court or in accordance with the terms of a debenture. Normally there is a clause in the charge which entitles the chargee to appoint a receiver.
3. An administrative receiver may be appointed by a creditor whose debt is secured by a floating charge on the whole or substantially the whole, of the company's undertaking. He or she takes control of the whole, or substantially the whole, of the company's property.

12.2.5 Effect of appointment of administrative receiver

1. The administrative receiver has sole authority to deal with charged property.
2. The directors continue in office but have no authority to deal with the charged property, so their role is extremely limited.
3. An administrative receiver is an agent of the company until the company goes into liquidation (s44(1)(a)).
4. The administrative receiver must, within three months of appointment, prepare a report to be sent to the company's creditors and must call a meeting of unsecured creditors.
5. Apart from any contract for which specific performance may be ordered, the administrative receiver may cause the company to repudiate any existing contract.

12.2.6 Winding up

Winding up (liquidation) is the process whereby the company's assets are collected and realised, its debts paid and the net surplus distributed in accordance with the company's articles of association. Winding up is followed by dissolution of the company.

12.2.7 Voluntary winding up

The members adopt a resolution to wind up the company (special or extraordinary). This may result in a members' voluntary winding up or a creditors' voluntary winding up.

a) **In a members' voluntary winding up**
   - the members of a company adopt a resolution to put the company into liquidation, following a statutory declaration by the directors that the company is able to pay its debts; .
   - the members appoint a liquidator, usually at the meeting where the resolution to wind up the company is adopted;
   - on appointment of the liquidator, all powers of the directors cease.

b) **In a creditors' voluntary winding up**
   - the members adopt a resolution to put the company into liquidation without a statutory declaration of solvency by the directors;
   - members can nominate a liquidator, but the liquidator must hold a creditors' meeting at which they may nominate a liquidator, who will become the liquidator of the company unless the court directs otherwise;
   - creditors may appoint a liquidation committee of up to five persons to act with the liquidator. Members may appoint five members to this committee.

12.2.8 Compulsory winding up

1. The court orders that the company be wound up on application to the court by a person entitled to petition. S124 provides that petitions may be made by:

- any creditor who establishes a prima facie case;
- contributories (shareholders who may contribute to the company's assets on liquidation);
- the company itself;
- the directors of the company;
- a supervisor of a voluntary arrangement;
- the clerk of the magistrates court if the company has failed to pay a fine;
- any or all of the parties listed above together or separately;
- the secretary of state;
- an official receiver – if the company is already in voluntary liquidation;
- an administrator of the company;
- an administrative receiver of the company.

2. The vast majority of petitions are by creditors.
3. The grounds on which a petition may be made are contained in s122 Insolvency Act 1986. The most important are:
   - the company is unable to pay its debts (s122(1)(a));
   - it is just and equitable to wind it up (s122 (1)(g).

12.2.9 Appointment of liquidator

1. The official liquidator attached to the court where the order is made will be appointed.
2. If there are substantial assets, an insolvency practitioner may be appointed to replace the official liquidator.

12.3 FRAUDULENT AND WRONGFUL TRADING

12.3.1 Fraudulent trading

1. Where a person (often, but not only, a director of a company) was involved in running a company which was operated with the intention of defrauding creditors, the liquidator can apply

to the court for an order that the person must contribute towards the assets of the company (s2131A 1986).

2. In addition to civil liability, the director may be disqualified under the Company Directors Disqualification Act 1986 or prosecuted under s458 CA 1985.

3. To establish fraud intention or recklessness must be proved (*R v Grantham* (1984)).

12.3.2 Wrongful trading

1. A liquidator may apply for an order that a director (defined as in s213) is liable to contribute to the company's assets if it can be shown that:
   - the company has gone into insolvent liquidation;
   - at some time before the start of the winding up, the director knew or ought to have known that there was no prospect of the company not going into insolvent liquidation; and
   - the director was a director at the time of the relevant transaction (s2141A 1986).

2. The director's conduct should be judged against the standard of a reasonably diligent person having both:
   - the knowledge, skill and experience that would reasonably be expected of someone carrying out the same function; and
   - the knowledge, skill and experience of the director himself.

3. One of the problems with these provisions is that if the compensation is paid, it usually benefits the holders of a floating charge, rather than the unsecured creditors, whereas the legislation was initially designed to help unsecured creditors.

CHAPTER 13

A NOTE ON THE COMPANY LAW REVIEW

The Steering Group of the Company Law Review published its *Final Report* on 26 July 2001. The Report is the culmination of three and a half years' work, not only by the Company Law Review Steering Group, but also by the Law Commission and the numerous individuals, organisations and professional bodies that have contributed to the consultation process.

Reference to the report has been made as appropriate throughout this book. In this chapter, an overview is provided and some of the recommendations not already referred to are mentioned.

13.1 OVERVIEW

13.1.1 Main objectives of the Review

The Review's main objectives are:
- to provide a framework to facilitate enterprise;
- to achieve consistency in the law;
- to achieve transparency;
- to achieve clarity and accessibility of the law.

13.1.2 Aspects of the law to be addressed

The Review recommends that the following aspects be addressed:
- complexity of the law (overformal language, excessive detail, over-regulation and complex structure);
- obsolescent and ineffective provisions;
- relationship between company law and corporate governance.

13.1.3 Key issues

The DTI identified eight key issues for the Review Panel:
- the scope of company law;
- the needs of small, closely-held companies – 'Think small first' has been a guiding principle of the Steering Group;
- regulatory and self-regulatory bodies;
- international aspects of company law;
- company formation;
- company powers;
- capital maintenance;
- electronic communications and information.

13.2 MAIN RECOMMENDATIONS

13.2.1 Small companies

One of the overriding principles has been to consider the needs of small companies. The Steering Group makes the following recommendations.

1. Decision making should be simplified for small companies.
2. Procedures should be streamlined so that private companies would not need to:
   - hold annual general meetings;
   - lay accounts or appoint auditors;
   - appoint a secretary.
3. An arbitration scheme should be created to deal with shareholder disputes.
4. The burden of financial reporting and audit should be reduced.
5. The rules on maintenance of capital should be simplified and the rules on prohibition of financial assistance for acquisition of shares in private companies should be abolished.

13.2.2 Company law institutional changes

It is proposed to set up:

- a Company Law and Reporting Commission to keep company law under review;
- a Standards Board to make detailed rules on accounting and audit and to provide guidance on the Combined Code;
- a Private Companies Committee to examine the impact of the law on private companies;
- a Reporting Review Panel to review reports and accounts of public and large private companies.

13.2.3 Next steps

It is unlikely that further progress will be made until 2002 at the earliest. A White Paper is likely to be produced in due course and new legislation is unlikely for several years – 2004 has been suggested. When it comes, the legislation will be in plain English and intelligible to business people and will replace the Companies Act 1985.

INDEX

UNIVERSITY
OF BRISTOL
LIBRARY

ENGINEERING